Margaret H. Bonham

Soft Coated Wheaten Terriers

Everything about Purchase, Care, Feeding, and Housing

Filled with Full-color Photographs

Illustrations by Michele Earle-Bridges

BARRON'S

2 CONTENTS

UNDERSTANDING THE SOFT COATED WHEATEN TERRIER

Meeting a Friend for Life

What is so special about the Soft Coated Wheaten Terrier? When you first see one, perhaps you are drawn to the striking wheaten open coat that gives this dog its name or its mild manner or outgoing disposition. Later, as you become more familiar with the breed, your viewpoint tends to shift from looking at a dog to looking at an individual. You find yourself treating the Wheaten more as a member of your family than as a family pet. Such is the power of the Soft Coated Wheaten Terrier. Wheaten breeders are fanatical in their devotion to this breed, and the overwhelming devotion to these jovial dogs is returned ten-fold by the Wheatens themselves.

The Soft Coated Wheaten Terrier is a happy, friendly dog of medium height and weight. While the American Kennel Club (AKC) classifies it as a terrier breed, the Wheaten is generally milder and less scrappy than most of its terrier cousins. Its roots are deep and steeped in Irish tradition, but it is not the dog of nobility. It is the dog of the common Irishman, the farmer, the herder, and the huntsman who needed a hardy dog to fill many roles.

The Soft Coated Wheaten Terrier is the Peter Pan of dog breeds.

Today the Wheaten enjoys its status as a companion dog. Gone are the days when it hunted vermin around the Irish farms and helped its master pursue quarry. The Soft Coated Wheaten Terrier is as comfortable on the couch beside its family members as it was on the misty hills of the Emerald Isle. If you open your home to a Soft Coated Wheaten Terrier, these dogs will open their hearts to you.

A Leprechaun in Disguise

The Soft Coated Wheaten Terrier is the Peter Pan dog of the terrier breeds. Always looking for something new and exciting, always happy and jovial, it is the dog that simply will not grow up. With warm and friendly personalities—and impish humor—one can imagine Wheatens as leprechauns in disguise. Wheatens constantly delight and frustrate their owners with new antics. Like small children they love and trust everyone—and will go home with the nearest stranger as easily as going home with you. Although they have mild and less aggressive temperaments, Wheatens can best be described as "active." They must be in the center of activity at all times, and if there is nothing going on they will come up with something to do. If it is not something you've planned, they will plan it.

Mischief can be their middle name. Wheatens make poor kennel dogs, requiring constant human interaction.

General Positive and Negative Traits

✔ A common Wheaten trait is jumping straight up and kissing a person on the face in a heartfelt welcome. Wheatens will greet both strangers and longtime friends in this manner. An exuberant Wheaten can knock down small children and muddy good clothing in little time. It is difficult to train a Wheaten not to do this, but it can be done if started early and if the dog is consistently trained not to jump up.

✔ Wheatens are not outdoor dogs. Although they enjoy the outdoors, their beautiful coat becomes a magnet for twigs, leaves, and dirt. Their coats quickly mat, even if groomed meticulously. Snow sticks to their coats in huge clumps, and rain quickly tangles and mats the hair. They are high-maintenance dogs, requiring frequent combing and brushing, not to mention trimming.

✔ Wheatens are not great obedience dogs. They bore easily with repetitive commands and require a lot of "fun time" to keep training enjoyable. Off-leash obedience work is often confounded when the Wheaten discovers something far more interesting and runs off to investigate. Many Wheatens have embarrassed their owners at obedience trials.

Caution: Never let a Wheaten off leash in an unfenced area; they may also bolt through opened doors and into traffic.

✔ Wheatens are very sensitive dogs and empathize with their owner's moods.

✔ They do not take punishment well.

✔ They love to be with their owners and love to explore new things.

✔ They make good watchdogs, barking at ringing doorbells and the neighborhood dog as it walks by, but they do not guard. They are more likely to greet a burglar with an enthusiastic kiss than a growl.

✔ They are good with sensitive and gentle children, but should never be left alone with a toddler or small child.

You may hear that Wheatens are the hypoallergenic breed of the dog world. This statement is not completely true. While Wheatens do not shed, their dander, oils, and saliva may cause allergic reactions in sensitive individuals.

A Brief History of the Soft Coated Wheaten Terrier

The Early Irish Terriers

The Soft Coated Wheaten Terrier shares a common lineage with its cousins, the Irish Terrier and the Kerry Blue Terrier. While the nobility in Ireland kept Irish Wolfhounds and other hunting and coursing dogs, they forbade the commoner such privileges; the Irish farmer instead bred medium-sized terriers as farm dogs. These versatile dogs killed vermin, herded livestock, hunted quarry to ground, and alerted farmers to intruders.

One romantic legend claims that after the Spanish Armada's defeat, a single blue-gray dog swam ashore and bred with the native Irish wheaten-colored dogs, producing the Kerry Blue, a cousin to the Soft Coated Wheaten Terrier. Some claim this was a Portuguese Water Dog.

Regardless of the legend's validity, wheaten and blue terriers appeared in nineteenth-century dog shows as "Irish Terriers."

Descriptions of some of these early terriers included open or soft coats as well as the better-known wiry dense coats.

The Soft Coated Wheaten Terrier Becomes Its Own Breed

Although the Soft Coated Wheaten Terrier has its roots in the Irish and Kerry Blue Terriers, the Wheaten was not recognized by the Irish Kennel Club until 1937. (The English Kennel Club recognized the Irish Terrier in 1880 and the Irish Kennel Club recognized the Kerry Blue in 1922.) Indeed, the Wheaten may not have become a recognized breed had it not been for the efforts of Dr. G. J. Pierse, a Kerry Blue breeder, who recognized the outstanding qualities of the Wheatens. Two breed clubs, the Irish Terrier and the Glen of Imaal Terrier Breed clubs, opposed the Wheaten Irish Terrier becoming a breed. Only when Dr. Pierse changed the name of the breed to the Soft Coated Wheaten Terrier were both clubs mollified. The English Kennel Club recognized the Wheaten in 1943.

Some of Dr. Pierse's dogs became the foundation stock of Maureen Holmes, the famed author of *The Wheaten Years*. Mrs. Holmes's dogs dominated in Ireland and her lines influence the Soft Coated Wheaten Terrier today.

The Soft Coated Wheaten Terrier in America

Seven Soft Coated Wheaten Terrier puppies arrived in Boston on November 24, 1946. These were the first Soft Coated Wheaten Terriers in America. Miss Lydia Vogel, of Springfield, Massachusetts, owned two of these dogs and proceeded to show and produce Wheatens in the United States. However, real interest in the breed did not develop until the O'Connors and the Arnolds imported dogs from Ireland in 1957.

The Soft Coated Wheaten Terrier Club of America (SCWTCA) formed in 1962 on St. Patrick's Day. Its founding members included the O'Connors, the Arnolds, the Mallorys, and the Wurzbergers. On March 17, 1973, the Soft Coated Wheaten Terrier achieved AKC recognition.

The Breed Standard

This is the official AKC breed standard from the Soft Coated Wheaten Terrier Club of America. See the SCWTCA's *Illustrated Soft Coated Wheaten Terrier Breed Standard and Amplification* (page 92, Information) for further details.

General Appearance: The Soft Coated Wheaten Terrier is a medium-sized, hardy, well balanced sporting terrier, square in outline. He is distinguished by his soft, silky, gently waving coat of warm wheaten color and his particularly steady disposition. The breed requires moderation both in structure and presentation, and any exaggerations are to be shunned. He should present the overall appearance of an alert and happy animal, graceful, strong and well coordinated.

Size, Proportion, Substance: A dog shall be 18 to 19 inches at the withers, the ideal being $18\frac{1}{2}$. A bitch shall be 17 to 18 inches at the withers, the ideal being $17\frac{1}{2}$. *Major Faults—* Dogs under 18 inches or over 19 inches; bitches under 17 inches or over 18 inches. Any deviation must be penalized according to the degree of its severity. Square in outline. Hardy, well balanced. Dogs should weigh 35–40 pounds; bitches 30–35 pounds.

These Wheaten puppies have warm and friendly personalities and impish humor. Be careful, one may steal your heart.

TIP

Wheaten Popularity

According to the AKC, Soft Coated Wheaten Terriers were fifty-ninth in registrations in 1998. Wheaten owners registered 1,988 dogs with the AKC, as compared to the 157,936 Labrador Retrievers registered in 1998. Wheatens are slowly growing in popularity, but are still a relatively unknown breed.

The Irish Coat Versus the American Coat

The American version of the Soft Coated Wheaten Terrier has a fuller and thicker coat than its Irish counterpart. The Irish coat is generally less "puffy," with a brilliant shine, and requires less maintenance than the American coat. There is some controversy surrounding the introduction of the Irish coat into American stock, but many breeders regard this as a necessity to preserve the breed.

Wheatens are a happy and jovial breed with warm and friendly personalities.

Wheatens can best be described as "active."

Head: Well balanced and in proportion to the body. Rectangular in appearance; moderately long. Powerful with no suggestion of coarseness. Eyes dark reddish brown or brown, medium in size, slightly almond shaped and set fairly wide apart. Eye rims black. *Major Fault—* Anything approaching a yellow eye. Ears small to medium in size, breaking level with the skull and dropping slightly forward, the inside edge of the ear lying next to the cheek and pointing to the ground rather than to the eye. A hound ear or a high-breaking ear is not typical and should be severely penalized. Skull flat and clean between ears. Cheekbones not prominent. Defined stop. Muzzle powerful and strong, well filled below the eyes. No suggestion of snipiness. Skull and foreface of equal length. Nose black and large for size of dog. *Major Fault—* Any nose color other than solid black. Lips tight and black. Teeth large, clean and white; scissors or level bite. *Major Fault—*Undershot or overshot.

Neck, Topline, Body: Neck medium in length, clean and strong, not throaty. Carried proudly, it gradually widens, blending smoothly into the body. Back strong and level. Body compact; relatively short coupled. Chest is deep. Ribs are well sprung but without roundness. Tail is docked and well set on, carried gaily but never over the back.

Forequarters: Shoulders well laid back, clean and smooth; well knit. Forelegs straight and well boned. All dewclaws should be removed. Feet are round and compact with good depth of pad. Pads black. Nails dark.

Hindquarters: Hind legs well developed with well bent stifles turning neither in nor out; hocks well let down and parallel to each other. All dewclaws should be removed. The presence of dewclaws on the hind legs should be penalized. Feet are round and compact with good depth of pad. Pads black. Nails dark.

Coat: A distinguishing characteristic of the breed which sets the dog apart from all other terriers. An abundant single coat covering the entire body, legs and head; coat on the latter falls forward to shade the eyes. Texture soft and silky with a gentle wave. In both puppies and adolescents, the mature wavy coat is generally not yet evident. *Major Faults—*Woolly or harsh, crisp or cottony, curly or standaway coat; in the adult, a straight coat is also objectionable. *Presentation—*For show purposes, the Wheaten is presented to show a terrier outline, but coat must be of sufficient length to flow when the dog is in motion. The coat must never be clipped or plucked. Sharp contrasts or stylizations must be avoided. Head coat should be blended to present a rectangular outline. Eyes should be indicated but never fully exposed. Ears should be relieved of fringe, but not taken down to the leather. Sufficient coat must be left on skull, cheeks, neck and tail to balance the proper length of body coat. Dogs that are overly trimmed shall be severely penalized.

Color: Any shade of wheaten. Upon close examination, occasional red, white or black guard hairs may be found. However, the overall coloring must be clearly wheaten with no evidence of any other color except on ears and muzzle where blue-gray shading is sometimes present. *Major Fault—*Any color save wheaten. Puppies and Adolescents—Puppies under a year may carry deeper coloring and occasional black tipping. The adolescent, under two years, is often quite light in color, but must never be white or carry gray other than on ears and

Illustrated Standard

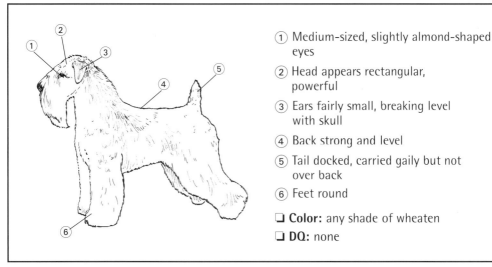

1. Medium-sized, slightly almond-shaped eyes
2. Head appears rectangular, powerful
3. Ears fairly small, breaking level with skull
4. Back strong and level
5. Tail docked, carried gaily but not over back
6. Feet round

❏ **Color:** any shade of wheaten
❏ **DQ:** none

*DQ = disqualification

muzzle. However, by two years of age, the proper wheaten color should be obvious.

Gait: Gait is free, graceful and lively with good reach in front and strong drive behind. Front and rear feet turn neither in nor out. Dogs who fail to keep their tails erect when moving should be severely penalized.

Temperament: The Wheaten is a happy, steady dog and shows himself gaily with an air of self-confidence. He is alert and exhibits interest in his surroundings; exhibits less aggressiveness than is sometimes encouraged in other terriers. *Major Fault*—Timid or overly aggressive dogs.

Approved February 12, 1983
Reformatted July 20, 1989

CHOOSING A SOFT COATED WHEATEN TERRIER

Are You Ready to Own a Soft Coated Wheaten Terrier?

Choosing a Wheaten—or any dog, for that matter—is a decision that should not be taken lightly. Sadly, numerous dogs suffer the same fate as other disposable items. Many dogs, including Wheatens, end up in animal shelters because their owners were not willing to take responsibility for their pets. Take this test to determine if you are ready to own a Wheaten:

✔ A healthy Wheaten will live on average 10 to 15 years; are you willing to rearrange your lifestyle to accommodate an animal that is dependent solely on you?

✔ The cost of a puppy does not end at its purchase price. Your Wheaten terrier will require ongoing food and veterinary expenses throughout its entire life. Puppies and elderly Wheaten terriers will generally incur more expenses than adults. Can you financially afford to care for your pet?

✔ Does everyone in the household want a Wheaten terrier, or any dog, for that matter? All members of the family must agree on a new pet.

These Wheaten puppies love being the center of attention.

✔ Who will take care of the Wheaten? Children cannot be depended on to take care of a living, breathing, animal; the Wheaten must be the responsibility of an adult in the household.

✔ Do you have a fenced-in backyard that is dig-proof, climb-proof, and jump-proof? Wheatens are terriers and will have a tendency to dig.

✔ Are you willing to take your Wheaten for a daily walk?

✔ Are you willing to go to obedience classes to train and socialize a puppy?

✔ Are you able to leave your Wheaten terrier alone no longer than nine hours?

✔ Are you able to give your Wheaten attention *every day?*

✔ Are you willing to put up with muddy paw prints on your clothing? Wheatens love to jump up and kiss their owners. This habit is very difficult to break.

✔ Is anyone allergic to dogs in your family? While Wheatens generally do not shed and are considered good dogs for those who have allergies, some people are still allergic to them.

✔ Are you willing to devote time to brushing your Wheaten several times a week and trimming it often? Wheatens are high-maintenance dogs that require frequent grooming.

✔ Are you able to tolerate the destructiveness associated with a dog? Puppies and dogs may chew the wrong things. You may find a hole in your garden where your Wheaten has excavated a new tunnel. Puppies don't come housebroken and the adult dog may have an occasional accident.

If you can truthfully answer each of these questions positively, then you are ready to purchase your Wheaten.

Questions and Answers

1. *Question:* Are Soft Coated Wheaten Terriers good with children?

Answer: Soft Coated Wheaten Terriers are easygoing by nature and will generally get along with considerate children; however, no dog should *ever* be left alone with a small child. Wheatens are known to jump up on people and may, in their enthusiasm, knock down small children. Any dog may bite, given provocation, and even a medium-sized dog such as a Wheaten can do a considerable amount of damage. Wheatens that are not properly trained and socialized or that are the result of poor breeding may behave unpredictably.

2. *Question:* Are Soft Coated Wheaten Terriers good watchdogs?

Answer: Soft Coated Wheaten Terriers will bark to alert you if something unusual is happening, but they make poor guard dogs as they consider everyone their friend.

3. *Question:* How time-intensive is it to groom a Soft Coated Wheaten Terrier?

Answer: Soft Coated Wheaten Terriers require frequent brushing and trimming. Because their coats do not shed, like double-coated breeds, they require trimming to keep their coats from growing too long. Their coats will mat without combing and brushing at least three times a week.

4. *Question:* Are Soft Coated Wheaten Terriers easy to train?

Answer: Soft Coated Wheaten Terriers are smart dogs, but due to their terrier nature, they can be stubborn and independent at times. You will find that your Wheaten will learn commands easily and then ignore them when it does not feel like obeying. If you are looking for an obedience OTCH Champion, don't choose a Wheaten.

5. *Question:* I am allergic to dogs. I heard that Soft Coated Wheaten Terriers are hypoallergenic. Is that true?

Answer: Wheatens do not shed the way double-coated breeds do, although some dead hair does come out while brushing them. Some people who are allergic to dogs find that they can tolerate Wheatens; however, the allergic reaction largely depends on the person. Some people are allergic to dog saliva, rather than the dog hair and dander. If you are allergic to dogs, it might be best to spend a few hours at a Wheaten breeder's kennel to determine whether or not you can tolerate a Wheaten Terrier.

6. *Question:* Do Soft Coated Wheaten Terriers require much exercise?

Answer: Wheatens are moderately active dogs and enjoy playing with their owners. They require daily walks and some exercise in the backyard, but are able to adjust to your schedule. The Wheaten is not a dog to leave out in the yard all day and does not need the intensive exercise some breeds require.

Puppy or Adult?

Most people prefer to purchase a puppy rather than an adult dog. There are several valid reasons for this. With a puppy, you start with a "clean slate": it hasn't learned any bad habits, it is ready for training, and it is very impressionable and will bond readily to you. However, raising a puppy takes much time and energy. If there is no one to socialize, train, and watch over a puppy during the daytime, consider purchasing or adopting an older Wheaten Terrier (see page 19, Buying an Adult Wheaten).

Older Wheatens will usually bond to their new owners as quickly as a puppy would, and many older dogs are housebroken and may know some commands. If a more mature and older Wheaten suits your lifestyle better than a puppy, then choose an older Wheaten. Try to find out as much as you can about the dog before you commit to purchasing or adopting it. Some dogs may have learned bad habits that you may have to break or may not be worth your time and effort. Still, there are many loving adults, both in rescue and from breeders, that are ready to be your faithful companion.

Male or Female?

Each Wheaten will have its own temperament, regardless of sex. Males may be more willing to please you, and females may be a little more independent, but these are generalities and temperaments vary between dogs. Choose the gender of your Wheaten based on your personal preference and your breeder's recommendations. If you have another dog, it might be wise to choose a puppy or dog of the opposite sex. While male and female dogs *do* fight, there is generally less aggression between the sexes than between two males or two females.

Show or Pet Quality?

If you are looking for a wonderful family member, a good friend, and an exercise companion, a pet-quality Wheaten Terrier is for you.

If you are looking to show your Wheaten in AKC shows and breed litters of outstanding puppies, then purchase a show-quality Wheaten. However, you should be aware that show-quality puppies usually cost much more than pet-quality puppies, and many breeders will not sell show-quality puppies to first-time Wheaten owners. Some breeders may have clauses in contracts requiring that the owners show the dog.

Does this mean that the pet-quality Wheaten is inferior to the show-quality Wheaten? Absolutely not! Show quality simply means that the puppy conforms closer to the Soft Coated Wheaten Terrier standard than other dogs. A pet-quality puppy may be a little too big or too small according to the standard, may have an incorrect bite, or may not have a correct coat. The reason most pet-quality Wheaten terriers are pet quality is merely cosmetic and does not affect the ability of the Wheaten to become a wonderful addition to your family.

Pet-quality puppies cost less than show-quality puppies because most breeders wish to offer a companion at a reasonable price. Reputable breeders require pet-quality puppies to be neutered or spayed because they do not wish the undesirable cosmetic trait to be passed into future generations of Wheaten puppies.

Buying a Puppy

Many dog owners purchase a puppy on impulse. Wheaten puppies, however cute, should not be considered impulse items, as

they are a 10- to 15-year investment. Puppies quickly become dogs and lose their charm. All Wheaten puppies are adorable, no matter where they come from. When you buy a puppy from a reputable Wheaten breeder, you have more than just a puppy; you have a puppy with a guarantee that it will be free of hereditary diseases. All reputable breeders will take the dog back anytime in the dog's life, should it be a puppy or a five-year-old adult.

Genetic Problems

Almost all breeds now have genetic problems such as hip dysplasia and progressive retinal atrophy (PRA). While the Wheaten Terrier is generally a very healthy breed, the breeder should have had the parents certified. Renal

Purchase your adult Wheaten from a reputable breeder or look for one through Soft Coated Wheaten Terrier Rescue.

dysplasia (RD) and PLE/PLN are three genetic conditions in the Soft Coated Wheaten Terrier that can prove fatal (see pages 59 and 80 for more information on PLE/PLN and RD).

Don't accept statements such as "he's had his hips and eyes checked" or "he doesn't have any genetic diseases." Ask for proof. OFA (from the Orthopedic Foundation for Animals) and CERF (from the Canine Eye Registration Foundation) are the two certifications; ask to see the *original* documents, not photocopies. Hip dysplasia is a crippling and painful genetic disease that may cost thousands of dollars to surgically correct. PRA and other eye problems can lead to blindness. RD often kills Wheatens before they turn three years old. Did the breeder have a veterinarian perform an ultrasound and a urine test? Ask to see the results.

Breeders

Contact the Soft Coated Wheaten Terrier Club of America, the national breed club for Wheatens, to obtain a list of Wheaten breeders in your area. You can obtain their address and phone number from the AKC (see page 92).

After you have obtained a list of names of breeders from a valid source, you must contact each breeder and ask some tough questions. The breeder, if he or she is reputable, will also be ask-

ing you questions. Look at the kennel facilities, meet the dogs, and determine whether a dog or puppy from the breeder's lines suits your needs. One thing to keep in mind: With the exception of a dam, which may be protective of the puppies, any dog in the breeder's kennel should be approachable. If the breeder is uncomfortable with you petting a dog, you may want to reconsider buying from that breeder. Aggression and timidity are major faults in Wheatens.

Too often, the buyer is more concerned over whether the breeder is "a nice person." "Nice people" are also known to run puppy mills, dump puppies into animal shelters, and breed dysplasic dogs. Puppy mill owners and backyard breeders are going to act "nice," because they

It's easy to look at a Wheaten puppy and fall hopelessly in love with it—ask for a breeder contract before looking at puppies.

Although pet quality and with a pet trim, this Wheaten's expression clearly displays why he is an affectionate and loving companion and in no way inferior to show quality dogs.

want you to buy their puppies. A reputable breeder may not seem nice because he or she is asking tough questions. The breeder asks tough questions because he or she cares where he sells the Wheaten puppies. He or she will often turn down ready buyers in order to find the best homes for them. This breeder will ask questions about you, your family, and your home. These questions may seem intrusive, but it is a sign the breeder really cares about the new home his or her Wheaten puppies are going to.

Finding a Reputable Breeder

✔ Does the breeder have only one or two breeds that he or she breeds? Reputable breeders focus on one or two breeds to improve the standard.

✔ Does the breeder belong to the Soft Coated Wheaten Terrier Club of America or to a local club? Wheaten breeders will be involved in the local breed clubs.

✔ Do the puppies' parents have conformation, obedience, or agility titles? A quality Wheaten should have or be working toward a title. If the parents are not titled, how close are they to obtaining titles?

✔ How did the breeder choose the stud dog? Was it a dog he or she had on hand or did the breeder search for the right dog to breed to his or her own female? The breeder shouldn t have bred his or her female to what was available, but rather looked for a dog that would improve the conformation and bloodline of the stock.

✔ Can the breeder provide photographs and information concerning the parents, grandparents, great-grandparents, uncles, aunts, and cousins of the puppies? If he or she cannot tell you about these dogs, then how is the breeder able to breed a quality Soft Coated Wheaten Terrier?

✔ Does the breeder have OFA and CERF certifications on both parents? A Wheaten's hips should be at least a *Good* rating, preferably *Excellent.* The CERF certification rating is either Passed or Failed. Ask to see the *original* certificates if the breeder has both parents. If the breeder has only the female, ask to see the original certificate of hers and a photocopy from the male's owners.

✔ Has a veterinarian cleared the parents of RD and PLE/PLN? Has a veterinarian tested the puppies for RD?

✔ Why did the breeder breed these two Wheatens? The answer should be to produce puppies that will improve the Soft Coated Wheaten Terrier breed. Often, the breeder will keep one or two puppies to see if they will turn out to be show prospects, but occasionally the breeder will not keep a puppy because they did not turn out the way he or she thought they would. Never buy a Wheaten puppy from someone who is breeding dogs to make a profit. Don't buy a puppy from someone who wanted a Wheaten just like his or her pet. The breeder should be striving to improve the breed, not breed pet-quality puppies.

✔ Ask the breeder for a contract. The contract is your bill of sale; the AKC papers are not a bill of sale. If the breeder does not have a contract, look elsewhere. The breeder should stipulate that he or she will take the Wheaten back under any conditions. The breeder should also guarantee the puppy free from illnesses, parasites, and hereditary defects. The breeder will stipulate that you must adequately care for the puppy and will require that you must never allow your Wheaten puppy to run at large. The contract should not have stud rights or requirements for breeding unless this is something you've agreed to prior to seeing the contract. The guarantee should not have a caveat such as strange diets or extreme limitation of exercise.

✔ Reputable breeders will not press you to buy a puppy. They will first try to educate you about what it means to own a Soft Coated Wheaten Terrier. They will tell you about the good points and the shortcomings of the breed. They may ask for references. Don't be insulted if a breeder sounds like he or she is grilling you. The breeder wants to be absolutely certain that this Soft Coated Wheaten Terrier puppy will fit in with your family and your particular situation. If the breeder tells you "there's only one left, you better buy it"— don't. There are other litters from reputable breeders.

✔ How old are the puppies' parents? Neither parent should be bred before two years old. They cannot have their OFA certification until that time. Breeding a Wheaten female before two years old is like getting a child pregnant— the female Wheaten is not ready emotionally and physically until two years of age.

✔ How long has the breeder been involved with Wheatens? Backyard breeders are usually new at breeding Wheatens, but occasionally you will find someone reputable who has this as his or her first litter, but who is also very involved in showing Wheatens.

✔ When have the puppies been wormed and vaccinated? A reputable breeder will either worm the puppies or have a veterinarian perform a fecal analysis on the puppies to determine if worms are present. Puppies should have received their first vaccinations at five to six weeks of age.

✔ When is the earliest the breeder will allow you to take a puppy? The youngest a Wheaten puppy should leave its mother is eight weeks old—no exceptions. The puppy must spend time with its mother and littermates to properly socialize it with other dogs. Before this time, the puppy may be very insecure and stunted in its emotional development.

✔ What items will the breeder provide when you are ready to take your Wheaten home? The breeder should provide you with: information on raising and training a Wheaten, the puppy contract, the AKC puppy papers, copies of the parents' OFA and CERF certifications, a sample of the puppy food the breeder has been feeding the puppies, a record of vaccinations and worming, a vaccination schedule, a pedigree, and any other information he or she thinks might be useful to a new Wheaten puppy owner. Some breeders may include a toy to help ease the puppy into its new home.

✔ Ask for references. The breeder should be able to provide you with names and phone numbers of other members of the Soft Coated Wheaten Terrier Club of America or local clubs and people who have bought puppies and who will gladly vouch for this breeder.

Buying an Adult Wheaten

Buying an older Wheaten is much like purchasing a puppy; you should also purchase your older dog from a reputable breeder. Sometimes breeders have an older puppy or adult that has not turned out the way they had hoped, and are looking to find a good home for this dog. Many times, the cost of these older dogs is lower because most people are looking for puppies. Use the same guidelines in searching for a reputable breeder as you would use for buying a puppy.

Shelters and Rescues

Sadly, some Wheaten terriers are dumped in shelters and dog pounds by owners who did not understand the level of commitment necessary to own a dog. These dogs may be perfectly good pets, waiting for someone with the patience and love necessary to train them.

The rescued Wheaten's background is unknown, as is its health record, but if you are willing to take that chance, in time and with patient training, a rescued Wheaten can make a loving pet. Be certain that when you do adopt such a dog, there is a clause in the adoption that states you can return the dog if a veterinarian finds the dog to be sick or unsound. Then take your new Wheaten to the veterinarian for a full physical examination, including fecal tests (for worms) and a hip X ray. If your Wheaten is older than two years, your veterinarian can tell you if it has hip dysplasia. Worms can be cured; hip dysplasia cannot.

Contact the Soft Coated Wheaten Terrier Club of America (see page 92 for the address) for a list of Wheaten rescue organizations near you.

The "Puppy Papers" or AKC Registration

All purebred AKC dogs have AKC registration, the proof that your Wheaten is a registered purebred. It does not mean that your Wheaten is somehow very valuable or more valuable than anyone else's is. It does not mean your Wheaten is show quality. It does not mean your Wheaten is healthy or well bred.

Breeders refer to the Puppy Papers as "blue slips." On one, you will find a place to fill in your Wheaten's name and your name, as well as a place where both you and the breeder must sign to indicate a transfer of ownership. The AKC now has a checkbox that the breeder may check if the puppy is to have a limited registration. If checked, this means that the puppy may not ever be bred and cannot have its litters registered under the AKC. In this way, a reputable breeder may indicate that the puppy is being sold to a pet home only. When you receive the registration back, it will have stripes on it, indicating that the dog is never to be bred.

Don't think that just because you have the Puppy Papers, your puppy is registered. It is not. You must fill out the appropriate boxes and send the form into the AKC along with the registration fee. Don't confuse the pedigree with the registration. The pedigree is the puppy's family tree. It may look very impressive with dogs that have strange registered names and the authentic

Wheaten puppies, however cute, should not be considered impulse items.

The adult Wheaten should be outgoing and friendly.

AKC gold seal, but again, it is not a sign of quality, nor does it register your puppy to you.

If you are buying an adult Wheaten, be certain that the breeder transfers over the registration papers as well. Depending on whether the dog is deemed show quality, the papers may either be a *full registration* or a *limited registration*. The breeder must sign the registration form to indicate a transfer of ownership. You must then sign the form and return it to the AKC with the appropriate transfer fees.

These papers, however impressive, do not constitute a Bill of Sale. They are not a contract between you and the breeder. If the breeder does not have a contract drawn up and intends to only use the AKC registration papers, you may want to reconsider buying a puppy or dog from this breeder.

Breeder Contracts

Before you even look at a litter of Wheaten puppies and fall hopelessly in love with them, you should ask for the breeder's contract. The contract should be anywhere from two to four pages long, stipulating the terms of the sale. Should you read the contract and not understand it, have an attorney look it over. Check out the following:

1. The contract should have a guarantee that the puppy or dog is free from genetic diseases and is healthy. Most breeders require the owner to take the puppy to the veterinarian between 24 to 72 hours after purchase to confirm the puppy's health. Guarantees for hip dysplasia and eye problems may have a time limit of two to five years and may have certain exclusions such as whether the owner bred the Wheaten before it was two years old. The breeder will usually refund all or part of the puppy's purchase price or provide a suitable replacement.

2. The contract should have what is called either "Right of First Refusal" or "First Right of Refusal." This means that the owner must first contact the breeder before selling or giving away the Wheaten. All reputable breeders will take back the dog they sold.

3. The contract will require that you will take adequate care of your Wheaten. You may be required to have a fenced-in yard or kennel and that you will not allow your Wheaten to roam.

4. If the puppy is sold as a pet, you may have to spay or neuter it before it reaches six months of age.

5. If the puppy is show quality, you may be required to obtain OFA and CERF certification before breeding it.

6. The contract should not have anything that limits your ownership of the puppy. You should never be forced into co-owning a dog, especially if you are paying a fair amount of money.

7. You should not be required to breed your Wheaten, nor to owe a puppy from some future litter back to the breeder. This is unfair to you because you shouldn't have to provide stock to this breeder, especially if you want a pet and not a show dog.

8. Finally, the guarantees should not have clauses that stipulate that the contracts will not be honored unless certain unusual conditions are fulfilled. Any conditions on the guarantees should be reasonable and not include

such things as bizarre homemade diets or limiting the amount of sensible exercise.

Choosing a Puppy from the Litter

When you are about to select a puppy, the first thing you should do is observe them. Are there any that are shy or timid? Is there a scrappy bully among the group? Is there one that doesn't show any interest in you, but instead wanders around looking to get into mischief? Is there one that is interested in your presence and happy to be petted?

You don't want a shy or timid puppy because it will most likely be shy or timid for the rest of its life. You don't want a scrappy Wheaten because it will be headstrong and difficult to train. You don't want an independent wanderer that won't listen to your commands. You want a puppy that is interested in you. Often, the puppy that comes to you first may be too dominant, so don't be fooled into thinking that it chose you. Instead, watch how the puppies interact. That will give you a good clue as to their personalities.

With the breeder's permission, separate each puppy you are considering from the litter and observe its reactions as you pet and cuddle it. At this point, the dam may become nervous or overly protective and the breeder may have to separate her from the puppies in order for you to perform your tests. Ask the breeder to do so if he or she does not.

Testing the Puppy

A normal reaction to being held and cuddled individually might be a little apprehension followed by cheerful acceptance.

✔ Gently place the puppy on its back and hold it there. It may struggle or yip for a few moments and then quiet down as you rub its tummy.

✔ If the puppy reacts aggressively by either trying to nip or struggling violently, let it go. This puppy is very dominant and may be difficult for you to train.

✔ If the puppy cries and submissively urinates, the puppy is too submissive and timid.

✔ You can further test a puppy by rolling a ball or tossing a toy. It should go after it eagerly and play, not shy submissively away from it or ignore it. Puppies have short attention spans so you may have to throw the object a few times before you get the puppy's attention. Clap your hands and call to the puppies. They should come over to investigate.

✔ Look at the puppies. Are they clean, bright-eyed, and well-cared-for? Are they alert and attentive? You may have awakened them from a nap, but they should still respond well to you. If the puppies act lethargic or cry piteously, you should perhaps consider another litter. Anything unusual, such as distended bellies, might indicate a problem.

✔ Finally, one puppy will no doubt be your favorite. Pick it up and snap your fingers behind its head. It should turn and look or at least respond. Wave a toy in front of its face and see if the puppy will try to grab it. While these tests are not perfect, they will help identify a deaf or blind puppy.

Choosing an Adult Wheaten Terrier

Choosing an adult Wheaten is different from choosing a puppy. A puppy is full of unknowns and surprises as it grows up; the adult is pretty much what you will see when you choose it. However, you should be choosing an adult that will have a stable personality.

✔ The adult Wheaten should be outgoing and friendly. Avoid any timid or aggressive Wheatens.

✔ The Wheaten may be exuberant, but should not be hyper when greeting you.

✔ If the Wheaten knows commands, walk it on a leash and practice the commands. Offer it a dog biscuit whenever it performs the command correctly.

✔ Call the Wheaten to you by clapping your hands. It should come readily at the sound of a friendly voice.

✔ Watch for any unusual behavior; if the Wheaten behaves in a different way than you expect, you may have to look elsewhere.

Questions for the Breeder About the Adult Wheaten

✔ Ask the breeder if the Wheaten is housebroken, crate-trained, and obedience trained.

✔ Find out from the breeder what bad habits the Wheaten has, if any.

✔ Ask the breeder why the Wheaten is available. If the dog is a returned animal, ask the breeder why it was returned.

✔ Ask for the name and phone number of the former owners and talk with them, if this is practical. Ask them why they returned the dog. They may be candid and tell you more about the dog you are considering.

Note: Don't be put off if the older Wheaten you've chosen has a name you don't like. You can rename it after you've brought it home; just be certain to stay with the name you've chosen so as not to confuse your new dog.

BRINGING YOUR SOFT COATED WHEATEN TERRIER HOME

What to Expect of Your New Wheaten

Puppies are adorable, but like all babies, they require attention. A puppy must be cared for, taught, and loved; it is not a toy that you can put away when you have finished playing with it. Be ready for the following:

✔ Expect sleepless nights from the puppy crying because you took it away from its mother.

✔ Waking up at 2:00 A.M. because the puppy has to go out.

✔ Missing lunch because you have to rush home from work or school to let the puppy out.

✔ Coming straight home from work or school because you have to walk the puppy.

✔ Chewed shoes, plants, books, furniture, carpet, and Sheetrock.

✔ Realizing that nothing on the floor is safe anymore.

✔ Soiled carpet; if your carpet is white or some other light shade, expect to replace it with a darker color that won't show stains as readily.

✔ Having to feed the puppy three times daily and walk it once a day.

✔ Brushing out your Wheaten's coat daily.

Puppies are adorable, but like all babies, they require attention.

✔ Arranging to care for your Wheaten if you go on vacation.

Wheatens require attention, love, and training, as well as vaccinations and regular veterinary checkups.

Where Will Your Wheaten Stay?

Before you bring your Wheaten puppy or adult home, you must first decide where it will sleep and spend most of its time. Wheatens are people dogs and will be unhappy if you leave them outside and away from their family. They may show their displeasure by nuisance barking, digging holes, or escaping. If you simply must have an outside dog, reconsider your decision about purchasing a Soft Coated Wheaten Terrier. While they are hardy dogs, they really belong inside with you.

Rusty and Bonnie: In order to avoid the rather impersonal "it," the names "Rusty" and "Bonnie" have been used throughout the remaining chapters to refer to a male and a female Wheaten, respectively.

Running at Large

When you let Rusty outside, you should not simply turn him out to run at large. Wheatens

CHECKLIST

The First Year's Cost of a Soft Coated Wheaten Terrier Puppy

The following is a cost breakdown of ownership of a healthy Wheaten terrier puppy during the first year. Be aware that illnesses and accidents can substantially increase this amount. These numbers are estimates only.

✔ Veterinary exam: $15 to $35.

✔ Vaccinations:

• Three sets of DHCPP, averaging $20 to $50 per vaccination.

• Two sets of bordetella vaccinations, averaging $10 to $25 per vaccination; optional unless the puppy is exposed to kennel situations or large numbers of dogs.

• Two sets of Lyme disease vaccinations, averaging $30 to $60 per vaccination; necessary in Lyme areas.

• One rabies vaccination, averaging $10 to $20.

✔ Worming:

• Puppy wormings: $20 to $50.

• Heartworm test: $10 to $30.

• Heartworm medication, one year: $50 to $100.

✔ Spay or neuter: $50 to $150.

✔ Puppy food, one year, approximately one 40-pound (18-kg) bag per month: $240 to $500, depending on the food.

✔ Dog crate: $50 to $200.

✔ Miscellaneous leashes, collars, toys: $100 to $200.

✔ Grooming equipment: $100 to $500.

✔ Visits to the groomer: $30 to $60 each.

are notorious for running away and will go home with anyone. Responsible dog owners contain their dog in either a fenced-in backyard or kennel run that is escape-proof. Dogs that run at large are a nuisance. They get into the neighbor's garbage, chase and kill wildlife, and may get run over by traffic. The city and suburbs are not safe places for a dog to run loose. Even in the country, there are many dangers for your Wheaten. Coyotes and mountain lions kill loose pets frequently, and farmers will often shoot strays that menace their expensive livestock. Dogs will run in packs and kill valuable game animals, forcing wildlife rangers to shoot the dogs.

Fences and Kennel Runs

If you can afford to fence in your backyard, do so. It should be a sturdy fence that is dig-proof, jump-proof, and climb-proof. A 6-foot (1.8-m) fence offers the best protection.

Necessary supplies you must purchase for your Wheaten: crate, bowls, bed, grooming table, toys, chew toys, flat collar and tags, leather latigo leash, nail cutters, and various grooming implements.

Household Hazards

Item	Hazard	Action
Children's toys	May cause obstructions or choking.	Keep toys out of reach.
Laundry	May cause an obstruction if swallowed.	Keep laundry out of reach.
Coins	Coins, especially pennies, may be swallowed, causing zinc or "penny" poisoning.	Keep coins out of your Wheaten's reach.
Household plants	May be poisonous.	Remove plants to a safer area.
Pesticides/poisons	Highly toxic.	Do not use in areas where your Wheaten goes.
Electrical cords	May cause electrocution if chewed.	Hide electrical cords; use specially designed extension cords that "sense" if the cord has been chewed through.
Antifreeze, windshield washer fluids in garage	Extremely poisonous.	Keep your Wheaten out of the garage.
Deicer for sidewalks	Caustic.	Use a pet-safe deicer.
Household cleaners	Poisonous.	Use children-safe latches on drawers and cupboards.
Glass tables, knickknacks	Can cut your Wheaten if broken.	Remove items out of your Wheaten's reach.
Toothpaste, medicines	Poisonous.	Keep out of reach.
Landscape plants	May be poisonous.	Keep your Wheaten away from landscape plants, or plant only nontoxic varieties.
Landscape gravel	May cause an obstruction if swallowed.	Keep your Wheaten away from landscape gravel.
Garbage pails	Your Wheaten may raid and eat items from it; may poison your Wheaten.	Put garbage pails in a cupboard under the sink; keep your Wheaten out of the bathroom.

Many people are unable or unwilling to fence in their property. This provides some unique problems for the pet owner. The best alternative to a fenced-in backyard is a kennel run. Kennel runs are relatively low in cost ($100 to $300), compared to fencing in an entire front yard or backyard. They do not have to take up much room and provide a secure outdoor place when you cannot exercise your Wheaten.

Electronic invisible fences keep a dog contained within your property boundaries, provided that you have trained him to do so, but they do

Never allow Rusty to run at large. He can get lost, get into trouble, or be hit by a car.

not protect him from loose dogs or from other dangers encroaching on your yard. The electronic invisible fences lose their effectiveness when the collar's battery dies or if Rusty discovers that he will not receive any more shocks once he leaves the boundaries. This containment method has its drawbacks, as you must first train the dog to respect the property line. You cannot install it and just turn him loose; otherwise, it will be ineffectual. These electronic invisible fences work best when there is someone at home who can train and periodically watch the dog.

Cables and Chains

Never leave your Wheaten tied up on a cable or chain; Rusty can quickly become tangled and severely injured. Dogs left alone on a chain frequently become frustrated and aggressive. Stray dogs can attack your Wheaten and children can tease it unmercifully.

Leaving Your Dog Unsupervised

Leaving any dog outside unsupervised is not a good idea. A lonely dog will bark and annoy your neighbors, causing them to call animal control and file complaints; neighborhood bullies will pick on your dog and tease him; unscrupulous people who hate dogs may poison your Wheaten; dog thieves look for pets for dog fighting and baiting aggressive dogs or for selling to an underground market for research. *Don't leave your Wheaten outside while you are not at home.*

Bonnie needs a crate, a bed, bowls, and chew toys to make her feel at home.

Always provide hard chew toys and treats to prevent destructive chewing.

Your Bedroom

Rusty will bond more closely to you if you put his bed in your bedroom. This provides eight hours or more time you are spending with him, even though you are sleeping, and will also help reduce his separation anxiety. However, Rusty should have his own bed, preferably in his own crate (see page 39 for a discussion about crates). There are several reasons for this, mostly dominance-oriented. You need to establish now that humans are above dogs. You will help avoid possible dominance problems by enforcing Rusty's sleeping area. Train him that beds are human territory only.

When Rusty cries for the first couple of nights, you can rap the crate and tell him to be quiet—all from the comfort of your own bed. If you are a light sleeper, you are unlikely to get much sleep the first few nights while both you and Rusty adjust to the new arrangements.

TIP

Providing Chewing Distractions

✔ Take a hollowed-out marrowbone and fill it with peanut butter.
✔ Fill hollowed-out solid rubber "indestructible" toys with hot dogs or bits of meat.
✔ Rawhide, cow hooves, pig's ears, smoked knucklebones.
✔ Nylon bones.
✔ "Puzzle toys" that allow you to hide treats inside.

Puppy- and Dog-proofing Your Home

Puppies and dogs find many things in the home extremely enticing. Use the Household Hazards table to check if your house is safe for your newest family member.

Other items such as newspapers, boots, shoes, and draperies may prove enticing to your Wheaten, and while they might not be poisonous, you may not want them chewed on. Always provide the appropriate toys and chewing items for your Wheaten so it will be less willing to chew something else (see below).

Teething and Chewing

All puppies teethe and chew; even adult Wheatens chew to keep their teeth clean and their gums healthy. Chewing is a natural instinct. You should provide suitable chew toys for your Wheaten, including large, hard rubber toys, heavy rope toys, nylon toys impregnated with flavors, and hard knuckle- or marrowbones. Rawhide and cow hooves make good chew items, but can come off in large pieces and be swallowed. Your main concern should be whether or not the item will cause an obstruction. Watch your Wheaten puppy as he chews a particular toy. If the pup manages to take it apart in large chunks that can still be swallowed, take the item away.

✔ Never give Rusty chicken, turkey, fish, or steak bones; they are sharp and splinter easily and can perforate an intestine.

✔ Soft latex toys are also dangerous, as Rusty can tear them apart and swallow the pieces. Keep in mind Rusty's chewing habits as you buy toys and treats. If you are not sure, purchase the most indestructible items and watch him as he chews them.

✔ Never let Rusty chew on clothes items such as old socks, pantyhose, slippers, or shoes. Don't allow him to chew on bedding or towels. You may not care about that particular item, but he will have trouble distinguishing between the old worn-out sneaker and your $200 pair of dress shoes.

When you find Rusty chewing something that you have not designated a toy, tell him *"No chew!"* and take away the item while offering something suitable to chew in return. Some people like to use the word *"Trade!"* You can say *"No chew, Rusty! Trade!"* and offer a toy or food for the item. Most Wheatens will gladly relinquish their prize if the item offered is more appealing (more on training beginning on page 37).

Choosing a Veterinarian

Choose a veterinarian before you purchase your Wheaten. A good veterinarian is well known throughout the dog-owner community.

Ask your Wheaten's breeder or other Wheaten owners for the name of a good veterinarian in your area. If they do not know any in your area, ask a dog-owning neighbor. If you are not satisfied with your options, you may have to consider looking up nearby veterinarians in the local Yellow Pages or obtain a list of practices from the American Veterinary Medical Association.

Once you have limited your search to two or three veterinarians, call them and make appointments to visit them. If you drop by unannounced, you may show up during a busy time when the veterinarian may not have time to talk with you. When you make an appointment, ask for a tour. The clinic should reflect the veterinarian's personality. Is it clean and well organized? Is the staff pleasant and courteous? Do you feel comfortable leaving your pet there? Ask to see the cages and boarding kennels, if the veterinarian does any boarding. Are the cages large enough for the animals housed? Are the runs escape-proof? Are they clean?

Ask the veterinarian about hours, both normal and emergency. Many veterinarians are on call for emergencies. If your veterinarian does not handle off-hour emergencies, you will have to bring your Wheaten to an emergency animal clinic, which can be quite costly. Finally, you should like the veterinarian. If you do not like him or her, you may not follow all his or her instructions, which may compromise your Wheaten's health.

Bringing Your Wheaten to the Veterinarian

Bring Rusty to the veterinarian for a full checkup before you bring him home. Bring any health and vaccination records the breeder or former owner provided. Your veterinarian may ask for a stool sample before your appointment. Collect the stool sample in a plastic bag and bring it with you.

When you give the veterinarian the stool sample and health records, he or she will most likely want to run a fecal analysis to check for internal parasites. If you have an older Wheaten and live in a heartworm state, the veterinarian may suggest a heartworm test and suggest that you put your Wheaten on heartworm preventative. If your Wheaten's vaccinations are not up to date, or if it is time for your Wheaten puppy's next series, the veterinarian will want to vaccinate your Wheaten and should examine your Wheaten for signs of disease.

Follow your veterinarian's advice concerning vaccinations. There are serious contagious diseases that puppies have no resistance to such as parvovirus and distemper. The mortality rates for these diseases are 50 percent or higher (for more on vaccinations, see pages 71–75).

You should also follow your veterinarian's advice concerning worms and heartworm (discussed more fully on pages 71–72). Worms will make your puppy sick and in many cases will cause malnourishment or even death, if left untreated. Heartworm is a deadly parasite that attacks the heart and pulmonary arteries. It is transmitted through a mosquito's bite. It is very expensive to treat heartworm, which is potentially life-threatening.

Should your new Wheaten prove to be unhealthy, contact the breeder immediately.

Use a travel crate to transport Rusty. He will be safer than running loose and will not interfere with your driving.

If you bought your Wheaten from a reputable breeder, the breeder may offer to pay your veterinary expenses, offer a replacement, or refund your money.

The Car Ride Home

When you pick up your Wheaten from the breeder, bring a travel crate to transport him to the veterinarian and then home. If you do not, Rusty may get agitated or carsick and interfere

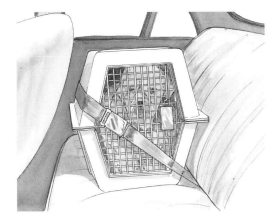

with your driving. Do not put Rusty in a cardboard box or other container where he can climb or chew his way out. Even if you bring another person to handle him while you drive, you should transport him in a crate.

Introducing Your Wheaten to Other Pets

Other Dogs

Wheatens are very outgoing and friendly and most can tolerate other dogs well. Still, there may be problems introducing your Wheaten to another pet. If you have another dog, the other dog may look on the new Wheaten as an interloper and may behave in unexpected ways including snarling and biting. Never bring a new dog home and leave him alone with your current dog. This could lead to a serious dogfight.

You may wish to reconsider purchasing a Wheaten if your current dog is much bigger than the Wheaten or usually shows aggression toward other dogs. Some dogs and breeds are naturally inclined toward aggression and fighting. That tendency will always be there, regardless of training or correction. Don't leave your Wheaten unsupervised with this type of dog; he may be severely injured or killed. A much larger dog will outmatch your Wheaten if a dogfight ensues. The choice is yours: Many large dogs are gentle and nonaggressive, but, as previously stated, regardless of whether or not you think your current dog will be friendly with your new Wheaten, never leave them together unsupervised.

Have a family member or friend bring your current dog on leash to a park and wait for you to bring Rusty there. Bring him to the park on leash and introduce them. Watch for signs of aggression: walking stiff-legged, hackles

Beautiful Wheaten Terrier puppies.

raised—when the hair on the back of the neck and shoulders stand up—hard stares, lifting or curling the lip, growling or snarling. Correct either dogs for aggression (correction is covered on pages 37–38). One thing to be careful of is to not hold the leash too tightly the first time you introduce the two dogs. You will telegraph your nervous feelings to your dogs and they will pick up on it and become nervous as well.

Assuming the first introduction goes all right, you should still not put the two together unsupervised for a while; there will be some sorting out to do as the dogs figure out their own "pecking order." Give the dogs equal affection; don't neglect your current dog because you have a new one. If your other dog acts aggressively toward your Wheaten or vice versa, seek the help of a professional dog behaviorist or trainer.

Your Wheaten puppy will quickly become a loving member of the family with gentle and consistent training.

Protect Your Wheaten Puppy from Deadly Contagious Diseases

While socialization is very important for your Wheaten puppy, take extra care during the first 16 weeks of his life to prevent exposure to strange dogs and diseases. Diseases such as parvovirus and distemper can infect a puppy even if he has had his shots.

Wait until after your Wheaten has received its final series of vaccinations before taking him to training classes, pet supply stores, boarding kennels, and dog parks. Don't allow strange people to pet your Wheaten puppy without washing their hands, and don't allow your Wheaten puppy to step through or smell strange dogs' excrement. You can further prevent tracking in parvovirus by mixing a spray bottle of one part chlorine bleach and 22 parts water and spraying it on the bottom of your shoes when you enter your home.

Cats

Introduce Rusty to the family cat at home. Your cat may hiss and scratch at the new addition, so be ready to keep Rusty from pouncing on the cat or chasing it. Correct any chasing or other aggressive behavior. While the Wheaten is not as scrappy as some terrier breeds, it is still a terrier and may chase the cat. Don't leave the Wheaten and the cat alone together. Eventually, Rusty may learn to ignore the cat and find other things more interesting.

Other Pets

Never leave birds, rabbits, mice or other rodents, or reptiles alone with the Wheaten. Don't introduce them or your small pets may suffer. Again, Wheatens are terriers and terriers were bred to kill vermin. Your other pets may be too tempting for your Wheaten. Keep your pocket pets in a safe place away from your Wheaten.

The First Few Hours and Nights

By now you should have chosen a place for Rusty to sleep and dog-proofed your home. When you bring him home, he should be naturally curious to investigate his new surroundings, but first let him relieve himself outside. In the excitement, this may take a while, but be patient; your Wheaten, especially a puppy, will have to relieve himself. Then bring him inside to explore.

Don't let the other family members swarm over your new addition; they may frighten him. Let each person quietly introduce himself or herself to Rusty with a pat or a treat. He may naturally greet everyone with jumping up and kissing. If this is not acceptable behavior, you can correct him gently by telling him *"No, off!"* and pushing him away.

Enforce all rules now. If Rusty is not allowed to get up on the furniture, do not allow him to walk over your new couch. If he is not allowed in certain rooms, gate those rooms or keep the doors closed.

Beginning Housebreaking

If Rusty starts sniffing and circling, immediately put him outside to relieve himself. Some

Wheatens may become so excited that they may forget to relieve themselves, but be patient and wait. Praise him when he urinates or defecates. If he starts to urinate or defecate inside the house, rush him outside and praise him when he relieves himself outside. Your surprise may be enough to correct it but you may add *"No!"* when you catch your Wheaten relieving himself inside. Clean up the mess immediately with a pet odor enzymatic cleaner or vinegar and water (for more on housebreaking, see pages 39–41).

Crying

Your Wheaten may cry the first few nights. If you keep him in his crate by your bed, you can rap the crate and say "No, quiet!" Eventually, he will lie quietly.

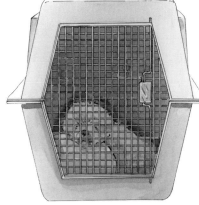

Use an old-fashioned alarm clock to simulate the rhythm of the mother's heart. A hot water bottle wrapped in towels will simulate the warmth from littermates.

TIP

Keeping Your Wheaten Puppy Quiet at Night

Some trainers recommend using a hot water bottle and an old-fashioned alarm clock to keep the new puppy quiet. The warmth from the hot water bottle is supposed to simulate your Wheaten's littermates while the ticking of the alarm clock is supposed to simulate the rhythm of the mother's heart.

✔ If you decide to try this, fill the hot water bottle with hot water and wrap it in a thick towel or blanket to prevent burning your puppy. Leave it aside for a short time and then put your hand on it. If it is very warm or hot to the touch, use cooler water.

✔ Put the wrapped bottle in the puppy's crate.

✔ Put the alarm clock, with the alarm shut off, on top of your puppy's crate.

✔ Before returning home with your puppy, ask the breeder for a washcloth or rag that has the mother's scent on it, and put that in with your puppy.

All these things might help calm your puppy, but never leave the puppy alone with these items; he might chew them.

Note: You may be able to substitute a heating pad for the hot water bottle; however, you should keep it at the lowest setting and keep the elements and cord well hidden from puppy teeth. Some pet manufacturers make chew-proof heating mats. Remember, you should never leave a puppy or dog alone with an electrical device.

TRAINING YOUR SOFT COATED WHEATEN

Training—Dog Psychology

Most Wheatens are very intelligent and sensitive dogs, capable of learning even complex tasks; however, many are easily bored with repetition and can be stubborn if handled improperly. Training is often no more than dog psychology. You, as the trainer, are trying to mold the behavior given a certain stimulus. When a Wheaten does not obey, it is often the trainer's fault, not the dog's—the trainer often has failed to communicate what he or she wants from the Wheaten. Once you learn how to communicate with your Wheaten, training will be easier.

Who's in Charge?

One way of learning to communicate with your Wheaten is to understand the concept of pack order. As you start training Rusty, you may hear about "alpha dogs." When trainers refer to the "alpha," they are talking about who is "in charge," who is "top dog," or "who must be obeyed." Dogs require someone in charge. They are pack animals and look to their owners for guidance. If the owner cannot provide suitable guidance, the dog seeks to become alpha. It is that simple.

All dogs are descended from wolves. In a wild pack, there are two alpha wolves, a male

Most Wheatens are very intelligent and sensitive dogs, capable of learning even complex tasks.

and a female. These wolves lead the other pack members. They lead the hunt, eat first, and quite often produce the only litter. They discipline and reward pack members. Often they are the strongest and the most assertive wolves. Alphas are born, not made, so any alpha offspring must either challenge the current alphas, submit to being lower-ranking wolves, or leave to establish their own packs. This system may seem unfair, but it is natural for wolves and dogs. There are many non-alpha wolves and dogs that are quite content to be led.

Praise, Correction, and Punishment

As Rusty's owner, you must become his alpha or risk losing his respect. This does not mean bullying him; you must be a benign dictator. Always be consistent in your praise and correction. Don't correct a dog for something one time and then allow it another time. Never punish a dog for something he does not understand or cannot do. At the same time, don't let him get away with things you know he shouldn't.

Never get angry at your Wheaten. Don't scream or yell when he has done something wrong, or you will quickly lose his respect; instead, teach him what you expect of him.

Often when a dog does something wrong, the dog does not understand or has misinterpreted what you have asked it to do. To punish a dog for something he does not understand is

CHECKLIST

Becoming Alpha

It's easy to assert your authority as alpha without too much effort. Try the following:

✔ Make Rusty sit while you fix his meal.

✔ Never free-feed; always establish set feeding times. It makes Rusty dependent on you for food.

✔ Eat your dinner first, then feed your Wheaten.

✔ Enter and exit all rooms first.

✔ Do not let Rusty sleep with you in bed.

✔ Put Rusty in down-stays while you are watching TV, eating dinner, or reading.

✔ Make Rusty earn his treats.

✔ Never play tug-of-war or rough-and-tumble games; they put you on the same level as your dog.

✔ Don't chase Rusty around the house if he has something you want; offer a treat and exchange the item for the treat.

✔ Never allow him to jump up uninvited on the furniture.

✔ Never allow him to "mount" you; this is a dominance maneuver.

✔ Take ten minutes each day to practice commands.

at the very best misguided. Never punish a dog for a mistake. The dog needs to be corrected and shown what you are trying to tell him.

This brings up the subject of correction. A correction is "anything that causes a dog to cease its current actions in a meaningful

manner"; it does not mean hit, kick, or yell at him. Correction must be meaningful in some way to your Wheaten; that is, the dog must associate his current actions with the action you've taken. The correction must also be effective, or it is completely meaningless. What you are trying to do is guide your dog into the appropriate responses given a certain set of conditions.

Setting a Schedule and Establishing a Routine

Dogs love a routine. It gives them something to look forward to each day and provides an emotional security that something remains constant. Even if you do not consciously establish a routine, Rusty will notice the times you wake up, go to bed, or feed him. After you bring your Wheaten home, you will want to feed, exercise, and train during certain times of the day. He will enjoy this.

Establishing a routine will also help train and housebreak your Wheaten. For example, if you let Rusty outside when you first get up, after you feed or exercise him, when you first come home from work or school, and before you go to bed, he will learn that those are the times he can expect to relieve himself. This will make housebreaking much easier.

Rewards

Always reward your Wheaten for good behavior. It can be verbal, a treat, a toy, or a pat on the head. Always be generous with your praise, but there can be too much of a good thing. Don't praise Rusty for his mere existence. Have him earn your treats and praise.

Likewise, never reward bad behavior. For example, never feed your Wheaten at the table or you will reward begging behavior. Keep food items out of reach or you will be rewarding food theft off the table or counters. If Rusty is not allowed on the furniture, don't allow him up on the sofa or bed "just this once." Dogs have remarkable memories and once you intentionally or unintentionally reward a problem behavior, you will be constantly trying to undo the problem.

Locating a Professional Trainer

Most novice owners and dogs can benefit from attending training classes. Often, your veterinarian will have a list of suitable professional dog trainers and behaviorists he or she can recommend. These trainers are generally not inexpensive, but will provide good results, and many will guarantee their training. There are many methods of dog training. Some are more negative reinforcement than others, so it is wise to first pay a visit to a training class to determine whether or not the instructor's methods are acceptable. If the instructor doesn't want you to watch for fear that you will steal his or her secrets, look elsewhere.

Choose a trainer who will train *you* to train your dog. Don't send Rusty to a training class where the trainer trains Rusty. Your dog will then look to the trainer, not you, to command him. Often, with behavior and training problems, the owner, not the dog, is causing them. The trainer is only training half of the equation when he or she is training just the dog.

Finally, choose a trainer you like and agree with. It is very difficult to learn from someone you don't like. Choose a trainer and method to fit your personalities.

Crate Training

Some people are adverse to crates because they look on them as cages; however, dogs have separate needs. Wolves and wild dogs have a natural denning instinct. They search for a safe place for them to sleep and raise litters.

A crate provides an artificial den for your dog. It is a place it can run to for security and know it will be safe. A crate is a safe place you can keep Rusty when you cannot watch him.

To get Rusty used to his crate, you will first wish to situate the crate in an active area, preferably out of the way in the kitchen or family area where he can watch your family, but still have a quiet place. Feed him in his crate. Put toys and treats in the crate to get him to enter it. Always reward your Wheaten with a treat when he goes into the crate when you ask him to. Use a recognizable word such as "crate," "bed," or "place."

Some adult Wheatens may have difficulty adjusting to crates, especially if they were not introduced to them as puppies. Very few may not be able to tolerate the crate at all, due to a past issue that you will never know. If you own such a dog, you may have to confine him in a small room or use an exercise pen, open wire panels that fit together in a circle.

Housebreaking

Housebreaking is the first big training challenge for the Wheaten puppy owner. Most puppies are naturally clean, not wishing to soil their sleeping areas. It is your job to teach your Wheaten puppy what is considered an acceptable place for elimination.

If you have not purchased a crate yet, consider doing so now. The crate will function as your puppy's "den" at least during its housebreaking phase. Once the puppy becomes reliably housebroken, you can decide whether or not the crate is still a useful tool for you.

Steps

1. Take your puppy for a walk or put him outside when you first wake up, after you feed and water him in the morning and evening, after you exercise him, during lunch, mid-afternoon, and before you go to bed. Keep to this schedule.

2. If you work or are gone during the day, do not leave the puppy longer than four to six hours without giving him a chance to relieve himself. An eight-week-old Wheaten puppy does not yet have the bladder control necessary for extended periods of time. If you have to leave a young puppy for a longer period of time, consider having a neighbor or a petsitter take him out for a walk. Some people will leave newspapers inside at the end of the crate or enclosed area so the puppy has a place to relieve himself.

3. Always praise Rusty for eliminating outside. You can use a command, if you'd like, such as *"Go potty!"* or *"Hurry up!"* Eventually, you will be able to have your puppy eliminate on command.

4. Watch your Wheaten puppy for any sign that he might have to eliminate. Such signs include sniffing and circling. If you see your Wheaten start to do this or start to eliminate, usher him outside.

5. If your Wheaten has an accident, show him the spot, tell him *"No! Bad dog!"* and show him where he needs to go. *Do not rub the puppy's nose in the excrement or hit him.*

6. To clean up the accident, use plain soap and water, followed by white vinegar and water or a good enzymatic-cleaning product. Do not use ammonia-based cleaners because these will not remove the urine smell and dogs will continue to soil the same area again if any smell remains. Follow the directions on the enzymatic cleaner for long-term deodorizing.

Exercise—the Key to a Well-behaved Wheaten

A tired Wheaten is a happy Wheaten and one unlikely to get into mischief. While Wheatens require less exercise than other terriers, they are still dogs and require some physical activity. Playing fetch or going on a long walk every day will help alleviate boredom. Practicing obedience, learning agility, flyball, or Frisbee will sharpen your Wheaten's mind and strengthen the bond between you. Problem dogs usually exhibit less undesirable behavior when they are focused on a particular task. Give your Wheaten something to do.

Teach Bonnie what you expect of her.

Always transport Rusty in a travel crate when he rides in the car with you. Never transport a dog in an open pickup bed.

7. Finally, be patient with your Wheaten. Some can be more difficult to housebreak than others, but if you set a schedule and keep to it, you will be successful.

Paper Training

Paper training is not a good method of housebreaking. It is slow and often confuses the dog about where it should eliminate. It teaches the dog that it is OK to eliminate in the house.

Some puppies are paper-trained by the breeder. If your Wheaten puppy is, he may become confused that you wish him to eliminate outside. Put newspapers outside where you wish your puppy to eliminate and take him over to them. Once your puppy eliminates, praise him. Eventually, your Wheaten will learn to urinate and defecate outside.

Housebreaking the Older Wheaten

If you have adopted an older Soft Coated Wheaten Terrier, you may find that it has not been housebroken. Do not despair! Housebreaking an adult dog is usually easier than housebreaking a puppy. Follow the steps toward housebreaking as you would a puppy.

Collars and Leashes—the Tools of Good Training

Before you begin formal training, you will need a slip-type collar, a flat collar, and a 6-foot (1.8-m) leather leash. You can purchase

Always reward Bonnie for good behavior.

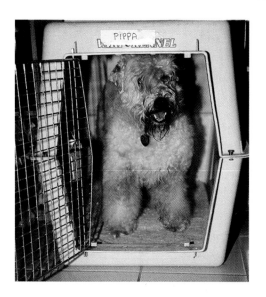

these items at a good pet supply store, through a mail order catalog, or at a pet store.

Slip Collars

The slip-type collar can be either parachute cord, soft braided cord, or chain. The collar should fit without any excess hanging down; if it does, the collar is too big. A slip collar must be put on properly or it will tighten on the dog and not release, thereby choking it. The best way to remember how a slip-type collar fits is that it makes a "P" when you place it over the dog's head. If it is a backward "P," the collar will not release properly.

Slip-type collars should never be worn in place of a flat collar. They should never have tags or anything dangling from the rings that will interfere with their function. Variations on the slip-type collar include the snap-choke, which is made from parachute cord and snaps onto the ring, and the prong collar. Both the snap-choke and the prong collar have specific purposes and should not be used in everyday training unless recommended by a professional trainer.

Flat Collar

The flat collar is your Wheaten's "normal" or standard collar. It should have the dog's identification and rabies tags affixed to it in some way. Rusty should be wearing a flat collar with tags all the time in case he gets loose. The flat collar should fit snugly around his neck; you should not be able to pull it off over his head.

Leashes

Use only a 6-foot (1.8-m) latigo leather leash for training. Do not use nylon, chain, or cotton leashes as they are hard on your hands and will hurt if Rusty pulls on the leash. You will want to purchase a 15- to 20-foot (4.6- to 6.1-m) cotton tracking lead or a flexible leash similar to the Flexi-Lead for recall training.

Problem Wheatens

Never allow a puppy to do something that is unacceptable as an adult. While this seems like common sense, many first-time puppy owners allow certain behaviors because they are cute as puppies. When the puppy grows up, however, the behavior is no longer cute and in some cases can be dangerous.

If you've adopted or bought an adult Wheaten with some behavior problems, you may have to consult a professional trainer for advice.

Mouthing and Nipping

Like babies, puppies are eager to pick things up. Because puppies do not have hands, they use their mouths to explore. While this may be cute and harmless as a puppy, an adult Wheaten that mouths is dangerous.

When your puppy begins to mouth you, rap his nose with your index finger and tell him *"No bite!"* If he insists on chewing on you, hold his lower jaw in your fingers without hurting him and tell him firmly *"No bite!"* Let go of the jaw. If the puppy does not attempt to mouth, give him a treat or toy as a substitution. Tell him *"Good dog!"* when he accepts the substitute. If he continues to mouth, repeat the above procedures.

Adult Wheatens that were never taught that mouthing is wrong may chew on hands or grab arms; occasionally, you will see one nip. If you have such a Wheaten, you can apply the same techniques as you would a puppy, but be aware that an adult may react unpredictably to resistance.

Digging

Terriers, being dogs that pursued their quarry to ground, love to dig. This instinct is common throughout the terrier breeds. The Wheaten still exhibits some of the same tendencies. If your Wheaten starts digging, you can stop it in various ways:

1. First, fill the holes with your Wheaten's feces and cover it with dirt; most dogs will not dig through their own feces.

2. Obtain empty aluminum soda cans and put some pennies in each. Crumple the cans so the pennies will not come out but you can still shake them and make a loud rattle noise.

3. Let your Wheaten outside and watch closely. When he starts to dig, go outside and throw a can toward the hole. Tell him *"No! Bad dog!"* The loud noise will startle him and discourage the behavior.

Never leave your Wheaten outside in the yard while you are gone. Most Wheatens are likely to become bored and may dig up or destroy plants.

Destructive Chewing

It is a natural instinct for your Soft Coated Wheaten Terrier to chew. Provide an adequate number and variety of chew items so Rusty will be able to satisfy this urge. Puppies, as they are growing up, will try chewing on everything. When you catch Rusty chewing on a household item, offer a substitute.

A properly fitting slip collar makes a "P" when you place it over the dog's head.

Some dogs become destructive chewers. This usually occurs out of boredom. If your Wheaten is a destructive chewer, evaluate when this occurs. Are you leaving him alone in the house during the day? If you are, you are inviting him to make your house his toy box. If the destructive chewing takes place when you are unable to watch him, crate him and provide a suitable chew item.

If the chewing takes place while you are watching him, tell him *"No! Bad!"* Then, offer a suitable item for him to chew. Praise him when he accepts the appropriate chew item.

Running Away (the Escape Artist)

If Rusty leaves your unfenced yard or runs off while off leash, don't allow him off leash in an unsecured area. As discussed earlier (pages 26–28), fence in your yard, construct a kennel, or take him on frequent walks while on leash. Wheatens are curious dogs and will usually roam if given the opportunity.

Teaching Your Wheaten to Walk on a Leash

1 Introduce your Wheaten to the training collar first. Put the training collar on your Wheaten and snap the leash to it.

2 Lure your Wheaten with a treat so the collar no longer tightens on his neck. Reward him for calm behavior.

3 If he struggles against the collar, try snapping the leash onto the flat collar. Just be sure the flat collar is tight enough and cannot slide over Rusty's head if he tries to back out.

4 Once you get Rusty outside, he will most likely be interested in the new surroundings. Let him lead you right now so he can get used to the feel of the leash and the upward pull on his own terms.

5 After Rusty is confident with the leash and collar, you can start taking him for short walks. Be aware that he will require some guidance in the direction you are going. Most puppies will tangle around you, trying to find interesting smells, or will pull like a sled team in the Iditarod. Either way, lure your puppy back with a treat, or you may give him a quick leash correction and continue.

The Escape Artist or Houdini dog will take every opportunity to get out. Careless owners frequently allow these dogs to devise new methods of escaping by putting up inferior barriers. The Houdini dog likes a challenge and has all day to figure out new strategies. The owner must provide a dig-proof, climb-proof, and jump-proof system in order to contain such dogs. Quite often, putting the Wheaten inside in a crate with a good latching system will take care of this problem.

Barking

Wheatens are not yappy dogs by nature, but any dog can turn into a nuisance barker. Most nuisance barkers are left outside and start by barking at people and animals in the neighborhood. Eventually, they bark because of habit.

Never leave Rusty outside while you are gone or while you sleep. If he barks while you are home, you can correct him by throwing soda pop cans with five to ten pennies in them. *Do not hit him with the cans.* Tell him *"No! Quiet!"* When he becomes quiet, tell him *"Good boy! Good quiet."*

There are bark collars and anti-bark devices available. Some work by producing a loud, unpleasant, and distracting noise; these do not always work, especially if you have a dog that enjoys barking. Others work with electric shock, providing a very unpleasant stimulus. A new collar on the market sprays a mist of citronella under the dog's chin. Dogs do not like the spray and cease barking. Of all the bark collars, the citronella collar is probably the most humane and effective.

Jumping Up

Wheatens are well known for jumping up. If this is a practice you do not like, put the Wheaten in a *sit-stay* and pet him only when he is in a *stay*. Also, when Rusty comes to greet you, order him into a *sit-stay* and then pet and reward him.

You will have a lifelong, loving companion if you train your Wheaten properly.

Separation Anxiety

Wheatens that suffer from separation anxiety will whine, cry, and bark when their owners leave, even for a little while. Quite often, the owner unknowingly encourages the behavior by making a big production out of leaving and returning. Never fawn over Rusty when you leave or return. Quietly put him in his crate and then leave. When you return, quietly let him out.

If your Wheaten already has separation anxiety, begin by putting him in his crate and leaving him with an interesting chew toy. He may whine and cry. *Do not rush back to correct him.* Instead, let him carry on until he has quieted. Then, when he is quiet, return and reward him for being a good and quiet dog. Eventually, Rusty will accept your comings and goings.

Occasionally, you will have a dog that will not fall silent and will continue to cry. If you have such a dog, consider contacting a professional trainer for help. Your veterinarian can also prescribe medications that may help reduce separation anxiety.

Dominance

Occasionally, you may be forced into dealing with dominance. Rusty may decide that he will challenge you for alpha or top dog. If you have been consistent in your training and your rules, you can put him in a *down-stay* and enforce it. If you have severe challenges such as growling or snapping, consult a professional animal behaviorist or trainer for guidance.

HOW-TO: COMMANDS

There are five basic commands every dog should know: *heel, sit, down, come,* and *stay.*

Learning the Heel Position

The correct position for your Wheaten to heel, sit, and lie down is beside you, on your left-hand side, facing forward. This is known as the *heel* position. When you walk your Wheaten, you should have the left hand holding the leash loosely to control the dog, and any excess leash looped in the right hand. This will give you the maximum control over a dog.

The heel position.

1. To put Rusty in the *heel* position, move him to your left side. When he stands or sits for a few moments in *heel* position, give him a treat and praise him.

2. Use a one-word command such as *"Place"* or *"Heel"* to mean *heel* position.

3. Practice putting Rusty in *heel* position and reward him when he stands or sits straight in that position.

4. Do not reward sloppily performed commands.

Heel

1. Have Rusty sitting beside you in *heel* position with training collar and leash on. Have a treat in your left hand.

2. Say *"Rusty, heel!"* and start walking, left foot forward. If Rusty starts to forge ahead or lag behind, get his attention by showing him the dog treat, and lure him into the correct position.

3. When he is in the correct position, praise him and give him a treat. If Rusty lags, pat your leg and encourage him to come beside you. If he forges ahead, pull him back using the leash, or have him focus on the treat and lure him back. Give him the treat when he is in the proper position.

4. When you stop, have Rusty sit in the *heel* position and give him a treat. When you start again, always start

with the left foot forward. Dogs see the left leg movement before the right leg moves. Also, it becomes another signal that he is to move with you.

Sit

1. Have Rusty standing beside you in *heel* position with the training collar and leash on.

2. With one hand, hold a treat over his nose, just out of reach and move it backward. With the other hand, lightly push down on his rump and say *"Rusty, sit!"*

3. Give Rusty the treat when his rump touches the floor.

4. Practice *sit* often and always reward when Rusty performs correctly.

Down

✔ Put Rusty in *heel* position with training collar and leash on and have him sit.

✔ Hold a treat level with his nose. With a swift movement, bring the treat to the ground closer to Rusty's chest and say *"Rusty, down!"* Rusty will hopefully try to follow the treat and drop to the ground. If he needs help to complete the *down,* you may lightly push on his shoulders.

✔ Give Rusty the treat only when he is in the proper *down* position.

Stay

1. Put Rusty on a leash in *heel* position and put him in *sit* or *down*. Tell him *"Rusty, stay!"* and move your outstretched palm in a sweeping motion toward his face.

2. Take one or two steps, *right* foot first, and turn around. If Rusty tries to follow you, say *"No, Rusty, stay!"* and move him back into his original position. Don't scold or act angry. You don't want him to break the *stay* because he is apprehensive. He will eventually stay for a nanosecond.

3. Before Rusty stands up, give him a treat and quietly praise him, *"Rusty, good stay!"* If he stands, put him back in his place. Wait a few seconds and if he stays, give him a treat again. Give him another treat before releasing him. Release him after he stays for ten seconds.

4. Continue working with him staying for only 10 seconds a few feet away until he has mastered it. Eventually, increase the time to 20 seconds.

5. Give Rusty treats while he is maintaining his *stay*. You will eventually increase distance and time, but do not increase both simultaneously.

6. You may be able to guess when Rusty will break the *stay* and be able to give him a treat before he breaks. Anytime Rusty shows nervousness or breaks his *stays* frequently, drop down to a shorter distance and a shorter time so he can have a successful *stay*.

7. Release Rusty from his *stay* with *"OK."*

8. Walk over and hug him for doing such a wonderful job.

Come

1. Start training *come* by hooking the 6-foot (1.8-m) leather leash to Rusty's collar.

2. Sit him in *heel* position, give him the *stay* command, and go out to the end of the leash. Remember to leave with the right foot. This is an added signal that lets Rusty know he is to stay.

3. Say *"Rusty, come,"* and give a little tug on

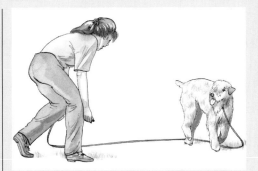

Teaching Bonnie to come.

the leash. If Rusty does not come, reel him in with gentle encouragement.

4. Clap your hands and repeat the command if you have to make Rusty come more willingly. Give him a treat the moment he arrives.

Once Rusty recalls reliably on a 6-foot leash, you can start lengthening the distance. You can accomplish this by using a long line, tracking lead or a long retractable leash. Practice your recalls in areas that have distractions. If Rusty can reliably come when called, you're both ready for the next step, which involves letting your Wheaten think he is off leash.

1. Put a light long line on Rusty with his leash so that when you take off the regular leash, you still have control, but Rusty is convinced he is off leash. When you do so, practice in a secure area.

2. Start from only 10 feet (3 m) away. Gradually lengthen the distance.

3. Once Rusty proves he is reliable in a secure area, move to an unsecured area with many distractions. If you ever have to use the long line, go back to the leash and work on his on-leash recalls.

Eventually, you will want to try your recall off leash. Again, practice in a secure area. If you have been doing your on-leash recalls faithfully, the off-leash recall should go smoothly.

FEEDING AND NUTRITION

Premium Dog Foods

Your Soft Coated Wheaten Terrier requires a diet that will provide all the necessary nutrients for energy and a healthy life. Bonnie will not thrive on table scraps, pizza, beer, or potatoes, nor will she thrive on cheap, bargain-basement, discount dog food. She will do best on a *premium* dog food manufactured by a *recognizable* company. *Premium* because you don't need to pay for fillers and protein sources your dog can't use. *Recognizable* because you don't want to drive halfway across town in bad weather because you just ran out of dog food. There are many good dog foods that are simply unavailable because one or two specialty shops stop carrying them.

Many think that all dog foods are the same since they tout similar protein and fat labels. They're not. Much of the difference has to do with the protein source and digestibility. An old leather shoe sole is high in protein, but how much of it is actually digestible? When you choose a premium dog food, you are paying for how much the dog can actually use—and how little you have to pick up in the yard on the weekends. Bargain brands often contain artificial colors, fillers, cute shapes, extra salt and sugars—all the things Bonnie doesn't need. What your Wheaten requires is a diet with a high-quality fat and protein source.

Neither puppies nor adults should be fat. This Wheaten puppy is active and fit.

Meeting AAFCO Guidelines

Whatever food you choose, it should have a statement that says "complete and nutritionally balanced" or a statement that the food meets the guidelines as set forth by the AAFCO (the Association of American Feed Control Officials) committee. AAFCO has established guidelines for dogs' and puppies' nutritional needs. Most major dog food companies comply with AAFCO regulations, but you should still check, regardless of the brand or manufacturer.

Ingredients

The first few ingredients in your Wheaten's food should include the protein source: chicken, beef, poultry by-products, lamb meal, and so on. This protein source should appear as one of the first two ingredients. Don't shy away from foods with by-products; by-products are an excellent source of protein and should not be overlooked. You should also consider "meals" such as chicken meal or poultry by-product meal, as they are simply ingredients with the water removed.

By-products: The quality of the dog food ingredients depends solely on the manufacturer. The definition of "by-products," for example, leaves much open for interpretation. Chicken by-products from one source may have a far superior quality than chicken by-products from another manufacturer, and some sources of by-products have better nutrition than the actual meat source. The AAFCO definition of meat, for example, can include heart and tongue, not just the muscle meat. Also, the AAFCO definition of "poultry" is broad. Don't be fooled into thinking that because you bought a dog food that says "poultry," it doesn't include livers or gizzards.

All-natural diets: Avoid "all-natural" diets that contain unusual ingredients, and vegetarian diets. Many have poor choices for preservatives and become spoiled quickly. While dogs can and do live on vegetarian diets, one look at the teeth of your sleeping carnivore should convince you that the dog was intended to eat meat, not tofu. Some dogs are allergic to soy, the primary protein source in vegetarian diets, which can cause stomach upset. Should Bonnie work in agility, flyball, or obedience with any regularity, you'll be switching to a meat-based brand anyway, because vegetarian dog foods have difficulty achieving a high enough protein/fat ratio. Many vegetarian diets have nutritional deficiencies. If you have a good reason for changing your Wheaten over to a vegetarian diet—for instance, if your Wheaten is allergic to meat—consult your veterinarian.

Table scraps: Table scraps are highly palatable, but usually high in fat, carbohydrates, and salt your Wheaten doesn't need. Table scraps and other such flavorings will turn Bonnie into a picky eater. Why should she eat plain old dog food when you'll load it up with all sorts of delectable treats? If you want to treat your Wheaten, save a couple of pieces for later and treat her separately, *after* she has eaten her normal food.

Supplements: Should you supplement Bonnie's diet with vitamins or minerals? In most cases, the answer is no. Your Wheaten's food should provide the nutrition she needs. If you choose to supplement, choose a balanced dog multivitamin. Do not supplement with a human dosage or single vitamin. Should she require supplementation, consult your veterinarian first and follow his or her directions. Supplementing can be dangerous and can cause imbalances or even toxicity.

Dry, Canned, Frozen, or Semimoist?

Dry Food

Pound for pound, dry dog food provides the greatest nutritional value for the money. It is often easier to store and is more convenient to feed than other forms. Dry dog food keeps relatively well, provided it contains a good preservative to prevent rancidity. Since most premium dog foods no longer use Ethoxyquin, a once common dog food preservative, these dog foods can spoil quickly if subjected to heat or long periods of shelf life. If your premium dog food is preserved with Ethoxyquin, it isn't necessarily a cause for alarm. To date, there is no scientific evidence to support the anecdotal allegations, which include everything from miscarriages and puppy birth defects to allergies. Although Ethoxyquin has been proven safe for years, dog food manufacturers are sensitive to public opinion and most have changed their preservatives to compete in the pet food market.

Shelf life: Most other preservatives don't have the shelf life of Ethoxyquin, so it is very important to buy *fresh* dog food. Most have a freshness or expiration date. If your brand of food doesn't, be sure you buy it from a store that turns their stock over regularly. Don't buy old bags—the food is more likely to be rancid and to have lost most of its nutritional value. A good practice is to buy a food no older than six months from the time the manufacturer produced it; most foods have a shelf life of one year or less.

Canned Food

Canned dog foods are more palatable than dry food, but are generally higher in cost. You are paying for the packaging and 60 percent or more water, making canned foods a very expensive option for the nutrient value. If you feed Bonnie only canned foods, she will have a tendency to have tartar buildup on her teeth, which can mean expensive trips to the veterinarian. Dry dog food will cause tartar accumulation as well, but not as rapidly. Some owners like to mix a little canned food with the dry food as a treat, rather than make it their Wheaten's sole diet.

Frozen Food

Frozen dog food is relatively new to the scene. It's harder to keep than dry and canned food because you must have enough freezer space. It's expensive too, since you are paying for water and storage, but it is highly palatable. Like canned food, it can cause tartar buildup on teeth, and because it does not have preservatives, once you thaw it, it can become rancid very quickly.

Semimoist Food

Semimoist dog food is usually high in sugars, soy, salt, artificial colors, and preservatives. The high amounts of sugar, salt, and preservatives are to maintain the semimoist consistency and still provide a decent shelf life. Stay away from feeding semimoist products, except as an occasional treat.

TIP

Home Diets

That bag of premium dog food in your pantry is the culmination of intensive research and testing. Most premium dog food companies strictly adhere to, if not try to surpass, the AAFCO guidelines for dog nutrition. Formulating a dog food is a careful balancing act, one that requires in-depth knowledge of such things as phosphorus/calcium ratios, fat, protein and carbohydrate percentages, and trace mineral supplementation.

With this in mind, how close do you think you can come to formulating a complete and balanced dog food at home? You can do it, but it is very difficult. If you want to provide your Wheaten a homemade diet, there are many good books available for formulating diets. Be wary of fad diets—many are improperly balanced, causing severe nutritional deficiencies. When in doubt, consult your veterinarian or canine nutritionist.

Whatever dog food you choose, choose a food formulated for the age and condition of your Wheaten. A puppy requires the extra nutrition of a premium puppy food. An active adult will thrive on an adult dog food formulated for active dogs. A senior or overweight Wheaten will benefit from a maintenance or "lite" type of dog food.

A word of caution: Just because your Wheaten is older does not necessarily mean

you should drop the protein. Years ago, veteri-narians used to think that high protein levels caused kidney disease. They don't, but this isn't a reason to increase her protein just yet. Your

A Wheaten puppy needs a premium puppy food to grow.

Wheaten must be active—agility, flyball, Frisbee, and so on—to use that excess protein to build and maintain muscles; otherwise, the kidneys will process out the unused protein. A high protein level will stress diseased kidneys, so if Bonnie shows any signs of kidney dis-ease, your veterinarian can provide her the proper diet.

Feed Rusty a balanced diet. There are many good high-quality premium dog and puppy foods available.

Wheatens need a premium dog food to keep them healthy and beautiful.

Palatability

Finally, buy a dog food your Wheaten likes. All the nutrition in the world isn't going to do your Wheaten any good if she won't eat it. The food must be palatable enough to keep her eating it day after day.

Note: Once you find a dog food your Wheaten likes, stay with that dog food. Don't switch brands or flavors for variety; that will make for a very picky eater.

Dog Nutrition Basics

Protein

Protein is a very important nutrient for dogs. Besides providing 4 Kcals—Kilocalories or "calories," as most people refer to Kilocalories—of energy per gram, it provides the building blocks necessary for formation of muscle, connective tissue, fur, nails, skin, blood, and organs. Protein is very important for growing puppies, active adults, and pregnant females. Older dogs require protein too. Don't limit your older Wheaten's protein unless he is obese or he has kidney problems. Your veterinarian can recommend an appropriate diet in those circumstances.

Protein can come from a variety of animals and plants. Animal protein is more complete than plant protein, meaning that it contains the correct balance of amino acids for a dog to live on. Plant protein in dog food usually comes from a variety of sources, if the diet is strictly vegetarian.

The AAFCO's minimum protein requirements are (for dry dog food) 22 percent for puppies and 18 percent for adults. Note that these are the bare minimum percentages; when you buy a premium dog food you are more likely to see protein levels somewhere around 25 percent to 26 percent for active adult dogs and 27 percent to 31 percent for puppies.

Fat

Fat is a wonderfully energy-dense nutrient at 9 Kcals per gram. Extensive research shows that canine athletes metabolize fat in a way similar to the way human athletes use carbohydrates. Dogs generally do not suffer from high cholesterol, so using animal fat is not a concern. Fat is also important in maintaining a healthy skin and coat. It provides insulation from cold and pro-

tects organs, and also carries fat-soluble vitamins such as A, D, E, and K.

High-quality fat sources include animal fat. Dogs use fats that are commonly referred to as Omega-6 long-chained fatty acids. They are usually a mixture of saturated (solid) and unsaturated (liquid) fats. Unsaturated fat tends to turn rancid more quickly. Typical fat sources include beef, poultry, and "animal fat," which may be a mixture of pork, beef, lamb, and horse fat.

The latest nutrition rage has been the Omega-3 fatty acids, touted for their overall health benefits. Common sources include a variety of fish oils and linseed oil. Omega-3 fatty acids are noted to help decrease the risk of developing certain kinds of tumors and cancers and have anti-inflammatory properties. However, there is too much of a good thing. Tests have shown that too much Omega-3 fatty acids can inhibit blood clotting in humans, and the potential for hemorrhaging if injured may be too great. Allow no more than 4 to 5 percent of the dry matter weight to be Omega-3 fatty acids. This does not mean you should dump your current pet food if it contains Omega-3 fatty acids; rather, you should be careful if you supplement or if the Omega-3 fatty acids are the primary fat source.

The AAFCO's minimum requirement for fat is 5 percent for adults and 8 percent for puppies. Most dog foods have more because it is an excellent energy source and makes the food more palatable.

Carbohydrate Sources

The most common carbohydrate sources in pet foods include corn and corn products, rice, and wheat. If your Wheaten is active, she will require fewer carbohydrates and more protein

Eggs

You may add a hard-boiled egg twice a week to Bonnie's food. Eggs are good for her coat and are a wonderful source of protein and fat. She will enjoy the hard-boiled egg (with the shell removed) crumbled over her food.

Foods to Avoid

Food	Result
Chocolate	Very poisonous to dogs; contains theobromine, which can kill a dog. Dark chocolate is more poisonous than milk chocolate.
Alcohol	Poisonous to dogs; because dogs have less mass than humans, it takes less alcohol to reach toxicity levels.
Raw pork	Can contain trichinosis, a dangerous parasite.
Raw chicken	Can contain salmonella.
Raw game meat	Can contain parasites.
Spoiled food	Will make dog sick.
Chicken, pork, fish, and steak bones	Can splinter or be swallowed whole. If you give your dog a bone, give her a beef knucklebone or a marrowbone.
Candy	In general, not good for your dog.

and fat. Some dogs have wheat or corn allergies, making barley, rice, or oatmeal an acceptable substitute.

To Free-feed or Not to Free-feed?

Free-feeding is leaving the dog food out all day for your Wheaten to munch on as she pleases. It's convenient for you because you don't have to establish a feeding time and all you have to do is make sure the dog food bowl is full. Don't do it.

Establishing a time to feed should be part of Bonnie's normal training. When you feed her, you are determining how much food she eats—not how much she *wants* to eat. At this time, you should make your Wheaten terrier sit (patiently) while you give her food (the reward).

You've established yourself as someone your Wheaten should look to for her food. You are teaching her good eating habits by having her eat when you put the food bowl down. Therefore, she is less likely to become a picky eater.

Finally, once Bonnie becomes used to her dinnertimes, it will be easy to notice when something is wrong. If she normally eats with gusto and enthusiasm, but suddenly picks at her food or turns up her nose at it, it is time to see the veterinarian. A sick dog will normally not eat and you can use her mealtime as a barometer of her health.

How Much and How Often to Feed?

Feed your Wheaten puppy three times a day at first and then two times a day when she

With so many bundles of wiggly Wheaten fluff, how could you ever decide which puppy?

Always provide fresh water from a good source.

Other Household Dangers

Human vitamins or medications should not be given without veterinary supervision. Some analgesics are toxic to dogs, even at low levels. If you want to give your dog a human form of medication, check first with your veterinarian.

Human toothpaste is poisonous to dogs if swallowed.

reaches four to six months. Her dog food should have feeding guidelines on the package, but be aware that those amounts are usually too large. To determine your Wheaten's needs, try those amounts first, split into two or three meals, then adjust accordingly.

If Bonnie picks at her food or ignores it when you put her food bowl down, leave the food bowl out for about ten minutes and then pick it up. Don't play with her and don't cajole her to eat; just let her pick at or ignore the food. If after ten minutes' time she has not begun to eat it, pick it up, and don't feed her until her next mealtime. Don't give her treats to "tide her over," and don't add table scraps to entice her. You want a puppy that will eat when you feed her what you feed her. For the next meal, she should get her normal food ration. Once she has finished eating, pick up the food and do not give her more until the next feeding time.

Changing Dog Foods

Occasionally you may have to change Bonnie's dog food. Perhaps it is because the breeder fed one type of puppy food and you want your puppy to be on another, or maybe it's time for your puppy to switch to an adult dog food, at about a year old. Whatever the

case, you need to switch over and you want to do it without causing diarrhea or an upset stomach.

Some Wheatens will get diarrhea if you suddenly switch their dog food. The best way to change your Wheaten's diet is gradually. Start her out with about 10 percent of the new food and mix it with about 90 percent of the old. Increase the new food by 10 percent while decreasing the old food by about the same percentage every couple of days. This should minimize her chances of having diarrhea.

Obesity

Neither puppies nor adults should be fat. Obesity can cause problems with joint and bone formation and can stress your puppy. You can tell the condition of your puppy or adult by placing your thumbs on her spine and using your fingers to feel her ribs. If you can't feel her ribs or spine or have a hard time feeling them through the fat, your Wheaten is obese.

Consult your veterinarian if Bonnie is too fat. Your veterinarian may prescribe a special diet that will help your Wheaten lose weight. Increasing her exercise also helps. An extra 15 minutes on her walk or a longer game of fetch may be all she needs.

Treats

Limit Bonnie's treats to no more than 10 percent of her normal diet. When you do give treats, they should hopefully be nutritious. Many treats shaped like human food have artificial colors, salt, preservatives, and sugar to entice both the owner and the dog. Use these sparingly, as most are very high in calories. A good puppy or adult biscuit by a premium dog food manufacturer is preferable to these since they are nutritionally balanced and aren't as fattening.

When you give your Wheaten treats, you will want her to earn them. Have her sit, lie down, give you her paw, yodel, or whatever before you give her the treat; she'll work much harder to please you the next time you ask her to do something.

Water

Water is the most important nutrient for your Soft Coated Wheaten Terrier. Although we don't think of water as being a nutrient since it is so commonplace, water is essential for life. Without water, Bonnie could die of dehydration in only 24 hours.

Always provide fresh water from a known good source. Water from streams or puddles can contain giardia, a microorganism that causes severe diarrhea, vomiting, and dehydration. Snow and ice hold very little water and you should not rely on them as a water source. Check your Wheaten's water bowl regularly and keep it full.

Dehydration can occur anytime. You can determine if Bonnie is dehydrated by pulling back on the skin behind the neck and releasing it. Normal skin will snap back. If a dog is dehydrated, the skin with stay where it is or will "melt" slowly back into position. The chapter on health that begins on page 69 covers dehydration in greater length.

PLE and PLN in Soft Coated Wheaten Terriers

Protein-Losing Enteropathy (PLE) and Protein-Losing Nephropathy (PLN) are two genetic conditions in the Soft Coated Wheaten Terrier. Dogs with these conditions may have skin problems that may otherwise be diagnosed as allergies. Common symptoms of PLE and PLN are vomiting, diarrhea, decreased appetite, weight loss, fluid retention, and lethargy. Wheatens with PLE/PLN may drink water and urinate excessively. Blood clots form in some Wheatens.

Veterinarians should test any Wheaten that exhibits signs of allergies or PLE/PLN. Wheatens that have this disease should be placed on a gluten-free (no wheat) diet with a novel protein source such as fish, venison, or other protein source not common in dog foods. Lamb is no longer considered a novel protein source because of its prevalence in dog foods. Some Wheatens show sensitivity to chicken, corn, and lamb. If your Wheaten shows any signs of hypersensitivity to such ingredients, your veterinarian can provide you with a hypoallergenic diet. For more on PLE and PLN, see page 80.

GROOMING YOUR SOFT COATED WHEATEN

Good Grooming Habits

Soft Coated Wheaten Terriers have single coats and are non-shedding. Their beautiful open coat makes them extremely high-maintenance dogs, requiring constant brushing and combing, on a *daily* basis in most cases. These fine coats will mat at the slightest opportunity, especially as the Wheaten grows out of his adolescent coat and into its adult coat. The Irish coat needs a little less maintenance compared to the American, but still is not a low- or even medium-maintenance coat.

Start learning the proper grooming techniques now. Train Rusty to become used to all the grooming early; it is much harder to train an adult dog. Teach him to sit or stand quietly on a grooming table while you brush, comb, or trim him. Get him used to bathing—he will need a bath once a month. Obtain the illustrated grooming chart from the Soft Coated Wheaten Club of America (see address on page 92) and learn what a proper Wheaten trim is.

Wheaten Terriers require brushing and combing a minimum of three times a week.

Even if you decide to use a groomer to bathe and trim your Wheaten—and many Wheaten owners do—you still will have the daunting task of keeping him mat-free and trimmed between grooming visits; otherwise, he will look like an unkempt blond sheepdog.

Grooming Equipment

A word of advice: Do not skimp on equipment. Cheap equipment can break and fall apart and the wrong piece of equipment can ruin the coat. You will need the following equipment, available from pet supply catalogs or at dog shows:

✔ Grooming table (arm and noose optional)
✔ Greyhound comb
✔ Pin brush
✔ Slicker brush
✔ Thinning shears
✔ Blunt-nosed shears
✔ Nail trimmers or grinders
✔ Mat splitter
✔ Mat rake
✔ Hair dryer made for dogs (human hair dryers are too hot for a Wheaten's hair and skin and can scorch)
✔ Tweezers or blunt-nosed hemostat
✔ Styptic powder

When Should You Groom?

Soft Coated Wheaten Terriers require brushing and combing a minimum of three times a week. Adolescent Wheatens between the ages of 12 and 18 months may require two or three brushings a *day* as the adult coat comes in. Wheatens generally need a bath and trimming about once a month. A show Wheaten will need more frequent grooming.

A Show or Pet Trim

Keep your Wheaten in a show or pet trim. An untrimmed Wheaten will become dirty and matted quickly; trimmed Wheatens are easier to care for and will have fewer health problems. If the prospect of trimming your Wheaten seems daunting, most Wheaten breeders will gladly teach you the proper way to trim your Wheaten.

Be certain the groomer knows the proper way to trim a Soft Coated Wheaten Terrier. If he or she does not, find someone who does. You owe it to the breed to keep your Wheaten in a recognizable cut.

Grooming Your Wheaten

Never trim or bathe a dirty or matted Wheaten. Bathing will cause the mats to worsen; trimming a dirty and matted dog will ruin the trim. Always comb and brush your Wheaten before bathing him and always bathe your Wheaten before trimming him.

Brushing and Combing

Start your brushing and combing session by looking for mats. Wheatens mat easily and you must first remove the mats before brushing and combing. You can remove small mats with the Greyhound comb or mat rake, but the larger mats will require a mat splitter.

How to trim a Wheaten.

Next, brush the hair against the natural lay. Part each layer to the skin and brush back from the skin outward, removing any dead hair and dirt. Do the same with the comb, thoroughly combing out your Wheaten's coat, layer by layer.

Trimming Nails

Wheaten toenails are very hard and grow very fast, so you must trim them weekly. Most Wheatens' toenails are dark, so you may have trouble seeing the "quick" or the blood supply to the nail. When you trim the nail, start cutting a little at a time. If you've let your Wheaten's toenails grow, the quick will be longer. Shortening the nail will cause the quick to recede.

Have styptic powder available in case you do cut the quick. The quick will bleed profusely. Pack the styptic powder into the quick with a cotton ball or ear swab and the nail will stop bleeding.

Ears

You should trim around the ears using shears, creating a clean outline. Us your fingers as a guide around the ear to avoid nicking or cutting the earflap. Next, use thinning shears to trim the hair on the ear to give it a natural, layered appearance. The hair should be very short on the tip, gradually becoming longer until it is about three-quarters of an inch at the fold.

Flip the earflap up and use tweezers or hemostats to pluck any hair from the ear canal. If you let the hair grow there, it quickly becomes a place for bacteria and wax to build up. This can cause ear infections.

Bathing

Wheatens need a bath about once a month. If you bathe Rusty too often, his skin will become dry. Use a good pH-balanced dog shampoo and conditioner. You can purchase professional dog shampoos and conditioners through pet supply stores and catalogs.

1. Before you bathe, brush, and comb your Wheaten, remove all mats. If he is muddy, allow the mud to dry and comb it out before bathing. Never bathe an uncombed dog.

2. As you wash Rusty, rinse thoroughly before applying conditioner. Any soap or conditioner in his hair will attract dirt.

3. Apply the conditioner and rinse thoroughly again.

4. Squeeze out excess water from the coat using towels.

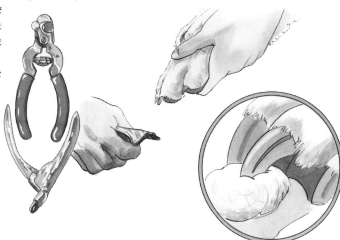

How to trim a Wheaten's nails.

Opposite page: The Soft Coated Wheaten Terrier is a medium sized, hardy, well balanced sporting terrier, square in outline. Above: The head is rectangular in appearance and moderately long.

5. Brush the coat using a pin brush, while drying the hair.

6. Set the hair dryer to Warm—do not use Hot—and brush out the coat while drying. (Hot dryers can scorch the skin and hair.)

7. Brush the coat against the grain so the dryer's air can dry the coat near the skin. Brush it back so it will lie properly.

Trimming

You can trim your Wheaten any way that suits you, but a shorter trim will be easier to care for. You can keep a shorter trim that reflects the Wheaten's show trim.

Use thinning shears wherever possible to trim. Straight shears will leave scissoring marks in a Wheaten's coat. When you trim, use your grooming table. Train Rusty to stand quietly on the table until you are finished.

Head and neck: The head should be rectangular, smooth, and blended with just a hint of the eye showing. Keep the fall long as it lies over the eyes; you may trim it in a V shape. Cheeks should be flat, not rounded or puffy. Use thinning shears. Keep a curved outline around the throat. Make the back of the neck neat with thinning shears.

Legs: Trim the legs with thinning shears to reflect columns. Trim all hair that doesn't present a clean line. Trim the hair between the pads.

Body: Trim so the Wheaten looks square when standing straight. Trim the belly so there is a proper tuck-up underneath and along the sides. Use thinning shears to blend the hair along the topline for a smooth appearance.

Rear and tail: Trim the rear so that the flank's appearance is neat and blends with the rest of the coat. There should be a tuck-up under the legs. The hip and hock should be defined. Trim the tail so it has a neat appearance. Trim around the anus for hygiene.

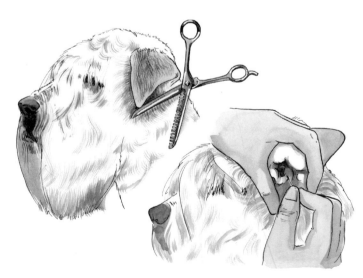

How to trim and clean a Wheaten's ears.

CHECKLIST

Grooming Recap

Soft Coated Wheatens have single, non-shedding coats that make them extremely high-maintenance pets. Regular brushing, combing, bathing, and trimming is essential to keep their luxurious coats in top condition.

1. Essential Equipment

To groom your Soft Coated Wheaten Terrier properly, the following items are among some of the most important tools you will need:

✔ A grooming table
✔ Combs
✔ Brushes
✔ Shears
✔ Nail trimmers or grinders
✔ Tweezers

2. When to Groom

The following schedules are recommended for pet Wheatens:

✔ Brushing and combing is required at least three times a week
✔ Adolescent Wheatens may need as many as three brushings a day as their adult coats grow in
✔ Bathing and trimming is required about once a month
✔ Trimming of the toenails is required about once a week

3. Grooming Basics

✔ Brush and comb your Soft Coated Wheaten before bathing
✔ Bathe your Wheaten before trimming the coat
✔ Thoroughly dry your Wheaten after bathing
✔ If you plan to show your Wheaten, you will probably want to consider using a professional groomer who knows the proper Wheaten trim

Please consult specific pages within this chapter for more information.

SOFT COATED WHEATEN HEALTH

The Soft Coated Wheaten Terrier is a hardy dog but, like all dogs, he can get sick or injured. Veterinarians can advise you about vaccinations, diet, and routine health care, but your Wheaten's health is largely dependent on you. You will be able to communicate more effectively with your veterinarian if you have educated yourself about what is normal and abnormal. Learn the warning signs of a major illness.

The Health Check

The best time to perform a health check is while Rusty is healthy. Take time during grooming to go over him. If you find something that feels strange, try feeling for it on the opposite side. Normal features are usually symmetrical. If you are unsure of what is normal, ask your veterinarian.

Head

Eyes: Are the eyes clear and bright with no signs of redness? There should be no excessive discharge. There should be no yellow or pus-like discharge. Dogs do not cry, so any tear may suggest foreign bodies or irritation.

Ears: Are the ears clean and free of waxy buildup? The skin color in the ears should be a

A beautiful, healthy Wheaten.

light pink, not red. Smell the ear—does it smell clean or does it have a foul odor? Dark red or black buildup may indicate an infection or mites.

Nose: Is the nose cool and wet to the touch? There should be no discharge. Dry and hot may indicate a fever. Your Wheaten should not be sneezing constantly.

Mouth: The gums should be pink and clean, not red and swollen. The teeth should be white. Look for broken teeth and teeth that have not come in properly; if Rusty is more than six months old, he should not have any puppy teeth. The tongue should be pink. Your Wheaten's breath should not smell bad; if it does, that may signal an underlying health problem such as gum disease.

Legs

Feel down each leg. You should feel no unusual lumps or bumps. If you find a lump, check the other leg to see if it is symmetrical. Elbows, pads, and dewclaws can be accidentally mistaken for tumors or bumps, so if in doubt, look at the lump. Move the leg slowly in its full range of motion. It should be fluid; if Rusty shows distress or there are any clicks, grinding, or catches, it may signal arthritis or joint problems.

Feet

Inspect the feet, both top and bottom. The skin around the toenail should be healthy, not red. The toenails should not be broken or too long. There should be no redness to the fur around the toes. Check the pads and between the toes for cracks, splits, and foreign objects.

Back and Ribs

Feel along the back and ribs. You should be able to feel the spine and ribs easily; if you are unable to, Rusty may be overweight. He should show no sensitivity to touch along the back and area where the kidneys are located. Feel for lumps along the side. If he hunches his back or shows sensitivity, it may indicate a more serious problem.

Belly

Your Wheaten's belly should be clean and free from dirt. Look for flea droppings and other parasites.

Note: Do not mistake the rows of nipples for ticks.

How to take your Wheaten's temperature.

Basic Home Veterinary Care

Taking Your Wheaten's Temperature

Purchase a digital thermometer that can be used rectally. Wash the thermometer with soapy water and sterilize with isopropyl alcohol. Use petroleum jelly as a lubricant and gently insert the thermometer into Rusty's rectum. Hold him quietly for about two minutes in order to obtain a reading. Do not allow him to sit down. Normal temperatures for Wheatens are 100.5 to 102°F (38 to 39°C).

Giving Your Wheaten a Pill

The easiest way to give your Wheaten a pill is to hide the pill in cheese, peanut butter, or a bit of meat. If your Wheaten is crafty, eats the treat, and spits out the pill, you will have to crush the medication and mix it with his food or give the medication yourself.

To give Rusty a pill, open his mouth and place the pill on the very back of the tongue. Close his mouth and hold his chin high while gently stroking his throat. If you place the pill in the right place, he should swallow it. If you find that you have to struggle to get the pill in, there are pet pillers that will safely deliver the pill. They are available at pet supply stores or in pet catalogs.

Giving Your Wheaten Liquid Medicine

Occasionally, your veterinarian may give you liquid medicines, many of which can be mixed in your Wheaten's food. If Rusty refuses to eat the food, you can give the liquid medicine manually. Slip your finger along his lower lip and use a spoon or a dropper to pour the medicine into the little pouch you've created. Gently close his lip and tilt his head back. Stroke his throat until he swallows.

Vaccinations

Your Soft Coated Wheaten Terrier requires vaccinations to protect him from deadly and contagious diseases such as rabies, parvovirus, and distemper. If you purchased your Wheaten puppy from a reputable breeder, he most likely had his first set of vaccinations when he was six to eight weeks old. Your veterinarian will probably vaccinate your puppy on his first exam and schedule appointments for vaccinations in a few weeks. Do not miss these appointments or your puppy will go unprotected, should the maternal antibodies fail during this period.

Colostrum Antibodies

Puppies receive their immunity during the first few hours of their life by nursing on a special type of milk called colostrum. The colostrum provides antibodies to protect the puppies against diseases for the first several weeks, then the maternal antibodies fade and the puppies become susceptible to diseases after this time. Veterinarians vaccinate puppies three or four times from about age 6 weeks to 16 weeks to catch the window between the time the maternal antibodies fail and hopefully before the puppy can become exposed to diseases. If a puppy is vaccinated before the maternal antibodies fade, the puppy will not be immunized.

Annual Vaccinations

Adult Wheatens require annual vaccinations for the same diseases as puppies. The notable exceptions are bordetella and rabies. If you board your Wheaten, or take him to obedience classes or shows, you should probably vaccinate him against bordetella (kennel cough). Some vaccines require twice-a-year inoculation; others are annual. Rabies is either a one-year or three-year vaccination, determined by your state health department. Follow your veterinarian's recommendations concerning vaccination schedules.

Internal Parasites

Worms

While worms are common in puppies, your Wheaten should be treated, as they can be dangerous for his health. Puppies can die from severe infestations. Worms make your Wheaten sick by living on nutrients meant for your dog or by living on your dog's blood. While there are many over-the-counter dewormers available, do not attempt to treat your Wheaten with them. Your veterinarian will provide the correct dewormer for your Wheaten.

Most puppies have worms, especially roundworms. Most breeders will worm their puppies before sending them home, but you should have your Wheaten rechecked for further infestations.

Worms infect puppies and dogs through ingestion of the worms' eggs. Eating raw meat from infected animals such as rodents, game, or infected farm animals can also infect dogs. Fleas carry tapeworms. The most common worms are roundworms, hookworms, tapeworms, and whipworms.

Signs: Common signs of worms include diarrhea, bloating, loss of weight or not gaining weight, bloody stools, anemia, and ricelike

Examine your Wheaten's ears for foreign objects or buildup that might indicate an infection.

flecks around the anus. Occasionally, worms can cause constipation. Wheatens that scoot on their bottoms are more likely to have impacted anal sacs than worms, but your veterinarian should check for worms anyway.

Heartworm

The heartworm is an internal parasite that lives in the heart, lungs, and bloodstream. Mosquitoes carry heartworm larvae from one

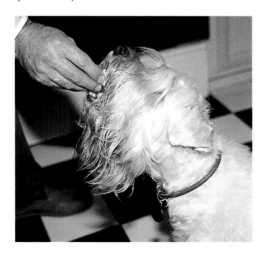

infected dog and inject it into another as the mosquitoes feed on blood. Heartworms will kill a dog. Most states in the continental United States have some incidence of heartworm. They are usually seasonal in the more northern states, so dogs from these states usually need to be on a preventive during the spring and summer months, while dogs from climates with mild winters need to be on the preventive year-round.

Veterinarians administer heartworm tests before putting dogs on a preventive to determine if they are already infected. If a dog is already infected, the dog must be treated for adult heartworms. There is now a new heartworm treatment called Immiticide that veterinarians administer intramuscularly, which is less risky and has fewer side effects than the old treatment. If your Wheaten has heartworms, be sure your veterinarian is using Immiticide or a similar treatment. Heartworm treatment is still risky and expensive, so it is better to prevent heartworm than treat it.

Preventives: There are many excellent heartworm preventives. Most are given once a month and may also control other internal parasites. Your veterinarian will first run a heartworm test on your Wheaten to determine if he has heartworms before prescribing a preventive.

Other Internal Parasites

Many other internal parasites can make your Wheaten very sick. The most common are giar-

The easiest way to give Rusty a pill is to hide it in cheese, peanut butter, or a bit of meat.

Your Wheaten relies on you to keep him healthy.

dia and coccidia. Your veterinarian can determine if Rusty has giardosis or coccidiosis through a fecal sample and can prescribe the proper medication to treat it.

Giardiosis: Originally confined to the Rocky Mountains region, most North American streams now contain giardia. Carried by wildlife, especially beavers, giardia are protozoa. Giardiosis can make humans as well as animals very ill. Symptoms include severe weight loss, diarrhea, dehydration, and vomiting. Several treatments may be required before giardiosis is completely

eliminated from the animal's system and symptoms may reoccur after several years. Puppies and adults can be infected. Your veterinarian may prescribe Flagyl or metronidizole.

You can protect Rusty from giardiosis by not allowing him to drink from puddles, streams, or ponds. Do not allow him in contact with wildlife and dog feces. Use bottled water in giardia areas such as mountains or rural towns where there are wells or inadequate water processing plants. If Rusty contracts giardiosis, pick up all feces to prevent reinfection.

Vaccinations for Contagious Diseases

Disease	Symptoms	Age Groups	Incubation Period/ Prognosis	Method of Infection/Primary Carriers
Rabies	Aggression, paralysis, choking, drooling	All ages; can be transmitted to humans	15 days to several months/100 percent fatal	Saliva through bites/inhalation/ foxes, raccoons, skunks, bats—any mammal
Distemper	Yellow-gray discharge from nose and eyes, high temperature, lethargy, appetite loss, diarrhea, dry cough, muscle spasms, seizures, hardening of nose and pads, depression	All ages, especially puppies and elderly adults	3–6 days/nearly 100 percent fatal	Airborne, or on clothing, shoes, or through direct contamination/ dogs, foxes, skunks, wolves, minks, and ferrets
Parvovirus	Severe diarrhea, bloody diarrhea, vomiting, dehydration, high fever, depression	Puppies and elderly dogs; usually less severe in adult dogs	7–10 days/ 50 percent fatal	Fecal matter; virus can live in soil up to one year/ dogs, puppies, foxes, coyotes, and wolves
Coronavirus	Severe vomiting and diarrhea, dehydration, fever. Coronavirus is often accompanied by parvovirus	Puppies and elderly dogs; usually less severe in adult dogs	24–36 hours/ less fatal than parvovirus	Fecal matter/dogs, puppies, foxes, cats, coyotes
Infectious Canine Hepatitis (ICH)	High fever, lack of appetite, excessive thirst, vomiting, eye and nasal discharge, jaundice, bloody diarrhea, hunched back, hemorrhage, and conjunctivitis	Dogs of all ages, usually puppies and elderly adults	4–9 days	Urine, feces, and saliva/dogs, puppies, foxes, wolves, skunks, and bears

Vaccinations for Contagious Diseases

Disease	Symptoms	Age Groups	Incubation Period/ Prognosis	Method of Infection/Primary Carriers
Leptospirosis	High fever, frequent urination, brown substance on tongue, lack of appetite, renal failure, hunched back, bloody vomit and diarrhea, mild conjunctivitis, depression	All dogs; can be transmitted to humans	5–15 days/ 10 percent fatal if not treated	Urine/rats, infected water supply, infected dogs
Lyme disease	Fever, lameness, loss of appetite, fatigue	All dogs; can be transmitted to humans	Varies/usually not fatal	Ticks/deer and mice are the primary hosts/dogs and humans
Bordetella (kennel cough) Canine parainfluenza virus; Canine adenovirus-1 (CAV-1); Canine adenovirus-2 (CAV-2)	Harsh dry cough; retching or gagging	All dogs	5–10 days/not fatal unless dog is very young, old, or is sick	Airborne and highly contagious/dogs

A new giardiosis vaccine is available that can help protect your pet from infection. Wheaten owners who live in high-risk areas should ask their veterinarian if they should vaccinate their dog.

Coccidiosis: Another protozoa, coccidia usually appear in large kennels, puppy mills, and areas where there are unsanitary conditions. Once introduced into a kennel environment, coccidiosis is very difficult to eliminate, so even reputable breeders may have trouble with it.

Your veterinarian may prescribe Albon to treat coccidiosis. Pick up all feces to prevent reinfection. Use a strong ammonia-based product, such as a pine cleaner, when cleaning up areas with diarrhea.

Fleas and Ticks

Fleas

Fleas thrive in all climates except the very cold, the very hot and dry, or in high altitudes. Their favorite spots for feeding are around your dog's ears, on his belly, at the base of the tail, and in the groin area. Fleas leave behind

black flecks that will turn red when they get wet. These are actually flea feces. Fleas can carry tapeworms and bubonic plague that can infect both you and your dog, if they are not controlled. Some dogs have an allergic reaction to flea saliva, which shows up as flea bite dermatitis.

Treatment: Consult with your veterinarian. He or she can recommend a good system for combating fleas. Some products, such as Program, available through your veterinarian and some mail-order pet supply houses, can break the fleas' reproductive cycle and reduce the amount of insecticides needed.

If you purchase over-the-counter flea and tick control products, be certain to read the warning labels for any possible interactions. Do not use them on puppies without first consult-

Follow your veterinarian's advice concerning vaccinations for a healthy Wheaten.

ing your veterinarian. Always follow the product's instructions. If you have questions concerning the possible interaction or poisonings, consult the hotline number on the product, your veterinarian, or a poison control center. There are several good flea-control systems by the same manufacturers intended to work together. There are also good systemic flea-control systems.

Do not use flea collars on your Wheaten. They do not work effectively. They can be chewed and swallowed and will poison your Wheaten. Also, ultrasonic collars do little to provide flea relief.

Ticks

Ticks carry numerous potentially fatal diseases such as Rocky Mountain spotted fever, Lyme disease, and Ehrlichiosis. Do not handle the tick or you may risk contaminating yourself.

Treatment: Use a good tick insecticide approved for use on dogs and treat the tick and the area around it. After you use it, wait a few minutes, then try to remove the tick with tweezers. Grasp the tick close to the skin and pull out slowly. If the tick's head or legs do not retract, do not pull the tick off. If you leave the head or legs in the skin, the tick bite can become severely infected. Wait for the tick to drop off.

The Preventic collar is a good tick collar, available through your veterinarian and some mail-order pet supply houses. It is very effective against ticks. If your Wheaten becomes sleepy after you put the Preventic collar on, remove it immediately and bring him to the veterinarian, as this is a sign of an allergic reaction.

Dental Care

Your Wheaten's teeth should be clean and white with no tartar buildup, and his gums should look healthy and pink, with no signs of redness associated with gum disease. Dogs seldom get cavities, but excess tartar will cause gingivitis. A diet that includes hard, crunchy biscuits and kibble will help keep tartar from forming on your Wheaten's teeth. Rawhide, hooves, nylon bones, rope toys, and raw knucklebones and shank bones will help keep your Wheaten's teeth clean and will massage the gums.

Teeth Brushing

Brush your Wheaten's teeth every week with toothpaste approved for dogs. Dog toothpaste is chicken- or malt-flavored and will not harm your Wheaten should he swallow some. *Do not brush your dog's teeth with human toothpaste;* the fluoride in human toothpaste is toxic and can make your Wheaten sick.

Most dogs do not like their mouth touched, so work slowly with your Wheaten:

1. First, get Rusty used to having his mouth handled. Gently hold his muzzle and flip back the gum, exposing the teeth. Praise him when he allows you to do this. Practice this often.

2. Once your Wheaten tolerates having his mouth handled, get a washcloth and wet it with warm water. Place your index finger on the washcloth's corner, holding the excess in your hand. Very gently, rub it along the gums in a circular motion. Always praise your Wheaten when he accepts this.

3. The next step is purchasing toothbrushes for your Wheaten. The best are the fingertip brushes made from either soft cloth or plastic. A conventional toothbrush can work, but will not provide as much control. Move in a circular pattern, not back and forth or up and down. With a little practice, your Wheaten will tolerate and perhaps enjoy this routine.

Dental Cleaning

If you brush Rusty's teeth regularly and provide enough chewing toys to keep his teeth and gums healthy, he will require minimal dental cleanings or tooth extractions. Veterinarians must anesthetize dogs undergoing dental cleanings. Anesthesia has risks; brushing your Wheaten's teeth does not.

If your veterinarian tells you that Rusty must have his teeth cleaned, make sure that he or she is aware of the anesthesia sensitivity within the Wheaten breed.

Illnesses and Injuries

Diarrhea and Vomiting

Changes in diet, overeating, strange water, and nervousness can cause diarrhea; however, parvovirus, PLE/PLN, internal parasites, rancid food, allergies, and other ailments can cause diarrhea as well. If Rusty is dehydrated (see Emergencies, page 81), has a fever of over 102°F (39°C), or has extreme or bloody diarrhea, bring him to your veterinarian as soon as possible.

Dogs vomit for a variety of reasons. Dogs vomit due to obstructions, an enlarged esophagus, parvovirus and other serious illnesses, allergies, and rancid food. If Rusty vomits frequently, projectile vomits, starts becoming dehydrated, or retches without vomiting, bring him to the veterinarian immediately.

If Rusty has mild diarrhea—loose stool with no mucus—or is vomiting without dehydration, you can give him a tablespoon of a Kaolin product (Kaopectate) and withhold his next meal. Encourage him to drink water or an unflavored pediatric electrolyte solution. If there is no diarrhea or vomiting, you can feed a mixture of boiled hamburger and rice at his next meal. If he doesn't improve, contact your veterinarian.

Lumps and Bumps on the Skin

Most lumps and bumps are usually benign sebaceous cysts; however, you should show any lump or bump to your veterinarian, especially if it is red, oozing, dark-colored, irregular in size and shape, or fast growing. If your female Wheaten has lumps on her mammary glands, have a veterinarian examine her immediately for cancerous mammary tumors. A large doughy lump on the stomach of a male or female could be a hernia that your veterinarian may have to fix.

If the lump grows rapidly and is painful or warm to the touch, it might be an abscess. Abscesses occur when foreign bodies such as foxtails enter the skin, or an injury closes up with bacteria inside it. Abscesses are serious infections. Your veterinarian must drain the abscess and prescribe antibiotics.

Broken Toenails

If you allow Rusty's toenails to grow too long, he may experience cracked or broken toenails. If the nail has broken below the quick, trim the toenail and file off any rough edges. If the nail is bleeding, you can stop the bleeding with styptic powder, silver nitrate, or an electric nail cauterizer available through pet mail-order catalogs. You can then paint the nail with a skin bond agent, which is available through veterinary supply houses or you can purchase it from your veterinarian.

"Hot Spots"

"Hot spots" are areas of moist dermatitis—skin inflammation—that may become infected. The symptoms are reddening skin, missing hair, and oozing woundlike lesions. Matted hair, allergies, or some other form of irritation frequently cause these hot spots. Clip all hair surrounding the hot spot and clean twice daily with a 10 percent betadine/90 percent water solution. If the hot spots are too painful, infected, or extensive, your veterinarian may have to anesthetize your Wheaten to clip the hot spot and prescribe corticosteroids and antibiotics.

Anal Sacs

If your Wheaten scoots along the ground or chews his tail or rear, he may have impacted anal sacs. These sacs usually express themselves when he defecates, but some dogs require frequent emptying.

To express these sacs, fold several paper towels or baby wipes together into an absorbent square. Place the square over Rusty's anus. With your thumb and forefinger press on the four and eight o'clock positions around the anus. The fluid is usually yellow or light brown and very smelly. The best time to express anal sacs is before a bath. Do not empty them too often or it might lead to irritation and impacted anal sacs.

If your Wheaten's anal sacs are not emptying and they feel hard and full, your veterinarian may have to empty them.

Ear Problems—Mites and Infections

To keep Rusty's ears clean and free from hair and waxy buildup, pluck out all hair growing inside the ears and clean them with a mild otic solution once a week.

A healthy ear smells clean and fresh with no waxy or dirty buildup and no redness. If Rusty's ears smell bad, or if he scratches at them constantly, he may have an ear infection or mites. Do not use over-the-counter ear mite solution, as the problem could be an infection and the medication may actually irritate it more. Have your veterinarian determine the cause and prescribe the appropriate topical antibiotic or insecticide.

Itchy, Scratchy Skin

Rusty could have itchy, scratchy skin for a number of reasons. If his coat is dull and dry, try adding a teaspoon of Canola oil to his meal once a day and a hard-boiled egg three times a week. If the coat remains dry, consider putting him on a hypoallergenic diet (see Food Allergies, page 81).

Flea bite dermatitis can cause itchy skin. With flea allergy dermatitis, the dog becomes allergic to the flea saliva. Eliminating fleas from him and your home will solve the problem and provide welcome relief. Your veterinarian can prescribe medications to alleviate the itching.

Mange mites can cause itching and hair loss. The two common types of mange are sarcoptic and demodectic. Sarcoptic mange causes intense itching, demodectic causes severe hair loss. Both must be diagnosed through skin scrapings and treated by a veterinarian.

Congenital and Hereditary Problems

Hip Dysplasia

Hip dysplasia is a hereditary canine disease that affects the formation of the hips. Hip dysplasia affects all breeds, including the Soft Coated Wheaten Terrier. The Orthopedic Foundation for Animals (OFA) reported that out of 3,414 evaluated Soft Coated Wheaten Terriers, approximately 4.8 percent of the Wheatens registered had either borderline or dysplasic hips. Most (73.2 percent) Wheatens registered had either excellent or good hips, so the chances of your Soft Coated Wheaten Terrier having hip dysplasia are relatively small. However, purchasing your Wheaten from a puppy mill or backyard breeder who does not screen for hip dysplasia may greatly increase the chances of your dog having hip dysplasia.

Hip dysplasia is potentially crippling and may be very painful. It is hereditary so no nutritional supplements will prevent it. In mildly dysplasic cases, your veterinarian may be able to mitigate it with antiinflammatories such as aspirin or nutritional aids as glucosamine. Serious cases may require expensive surgery. Some extreme cases of hip dysplasia may be so painful that the humane thing to do is to euthanize the dog.

PRA, CPRA, and Cataracts

Progressive Retinal Atrophy (PRA) and Central Progressive Retinal Atrophy (CPRA) are two degenerative eye disorders that lead to blindness. Cataracts or cloudiness of the eye's lens can be due to either hereditary or environmental reasons. Juvenile cataracts are usually hereditary.

A veterinary ophthalmologist can determine whether your Wheaten has these or other eye diseases. The Canine Eye Registry Foundation, or CERF, provides a registry for dogs intended for breeding. The CERF evaluation lasts for one year. Any Wheaten that you buy should have both its parents registered with CERF. If you plan to breed your Wheatens, you will need to have their eyes examined and have them registered with CERF.

Renal Dysplasia (RD)

Renal dysplasia (or juvenile renal dysplasia) is a genetic disease in Wheatens that affects the kidneys; the kidneys are malformed and unable to function properly. Clinical signs of RD usually appear in affected Wheatens between four months and three years old. Symptoms include excessive thirst and urination and can include vomiting, weight loss, and sometimes diarrhea.

Breeders should test their puppies for RD as early as eight weeks with an ultrasound and a urine test. A renal biopsy may be more accurate, but it is more invasive. If your breeder did not test your Wheaten for RD, you may want to have your veterinarian perform an ultrasound and a urine test to determine if the dog has this problem. The prognosis is not good for a long life, but your veterinarian can recommend a special low-protein diet and a course of treatment.

VetGen, a bio research company dedicated to researching diseases affecting purebred animals, and the University of Michigan are currently researching the genes that cause RD.

Protein-Losing Enteropathy (PLE) and Protein-Losing Nephropathy (PLN)

PLE/PLN is a condition in which either the intestines or the kidneys are unable to process protein correctly and actually lose protein. Unlike RD, PLE/PLN can occur anytime during the Wheaten's life and cannot be reliably screened for until the clinical signs are present. PLE/PLN is a genetic disease, but the mode of inheritance is unknown. Dogs with PLE or PLN will lose weight, show food allergies, and have diarrhea and vomiting. Veterinarians can diagnose PLE or PLN with a blood chemistry and urine test.

If there is a relationship between RD and PLE/PLN, it is currently unknown. More Wheatens have PLE/PLN than RD, and PLE/PLN may suddenly appear in lines that breeders thought to be free from it. Breeders try to screen for the disease, but it may appear in middle-aged or older dogs that have already been bred several times and produced puppies; therefore, a perfectly normal puppy from a reputable breeder may have PLE or PLN.

If your veterinarian diagnoses your Wheaten as having either PLE or PLN, he or she may prescribe a hypoallergenic diet that is wheat-free and has a novel protein source (see Food Allergies, below, for more information).

Food Allergies

Ironically, a common food allergy in the Wheaten Terrier is wheat or wheat gluten. Wheatens may also show allergies to corn, chicken, lamb, and milk products. These allergies may be a result of PLE or PLN or another genetic factor. Wheatens exhibiting food allergies may have itchy skin and dermatitis or may have gastric upset, weight loss, vomiting, and diarrhea. If Rusty shows any of these symptoms, have him tested for PLE/PLN.

Some dogs have shown allergies to lamb and rice diets. At one time, veterinarians and nutritionists considered lamb hypoallergenic because it was relatively unavailable as a dog food source. As lamb and rice diets have become popular, increasing numbers of dogs have become allergic to lamb. Your veterinarian can prescribe a diet with a novel protein source such as venison, fish, or turkey.

Anesthesia Sensitivity

Wheatens may exhibit sensitivity to anesthetics similar to sighthounds and northern breeds. Due to this sensitivity, you should make sure your veterinarian takes precautions.

Emergencies

Should your Wheaten become sick or injured, having a first aid kit and emergency numbers handy may save his life. In all emergencies, obtain veterinary treatment as soon as possible. Ask your veterinarian to show you how to perform CPR and mouth-to-mouth resuscitation on your Wheaten.

Muzzling Your Wheaten in Emergency Situations

Any dog when injured or frightened may bite. To avoid being injured during an emergency, have a muzzle handy. If you do not have a muzzle, you can fashion one from a long strip of bandage, a tie, or cord.

Start in the middle at the bottom of the dog's muzzle. Wrap the bandage upward, tie, and then bring it back downward under the chin and tie. Take the two loose ends and tie them behind the dog's head securely.

Caution: Do not muzzle a dog that is having trouble breathing.

Dehydration and Heatstroke

Signs of dehydration and heatstroke: The skin around the muzzle or neck does not snap back when pinched, elevated temperature, extreme thirst, watery diarrhea, vomiting, high temperature—over 103°F (39.4°C), difficulty breathing, lethargy, weakness, and pale gums.

Do not muzzle the dog. Move him into shade or cool and well-ventilated area. Give him cool water or unflavored pediatric electrolyte to drink. Soak him in tepid or cool water; ice cold water will cause the capillaries to contract and not dissipate heat. Make certain the dog can breathe; remove constricting collars or other items. Get him immediate veterinary attention.

Prevent heatstroke by keeping your dog in well-ventilated areas with shade in the summertime. Fresh water should always be available. Do not exercise your dog in hot weather. Keep him mat-free. *Never leave a dog in a car during warm weather even with the windows down.*

Choking and Difficulty Breathing

Signs include coughing, gagging, gums and

CHECKLIST

The First Aid Kit

Every household with a dog should have a first aid kit. You can assemble one from easily purchasable items:

✔ Large and small nonstick bandage pads
✔ Sterile gauze wrappings
✔ Sterile sponges
✔ Pressure bandages
✔ Self-adhesive wrap (VetWrap)
✔ Disposable latex gloves
✔ Triple antibiotic ointment or nitrofurizone, available through veterinary supply catalogs
✔ Bandage tape
✔ Surgical glue or VetBond, available through veterinary supply catalogs
✔ Cortisone cream
✔ Quick muzzle
✔ Rectal thermometer
✔ Unflavored pediatric electrolyte (Pedalyte)
✔ Syrup of Ipecac
✔ Betadine solution
✔ Bandage scissors
✔ Petroleum jelly (Vaseline)
✔ Mineral oil
✔ Kaolin product (Kaopectate)
✔ Aspirin
✔ Hydrogen peroxide
✔ Tweezers
✔ Your veterinarian's phone number, pager, after-hours number
✔ An emergency veterinary hospital's phone number
✔ Local poison control center phone number

tongue turning pale or blue, and wheezing. Do not muzzle; seek immediate veterinary attention. Loosen the collar and anything else that might restrict breathing. Check your Wheaten's throat for any object caught in the throat. If you see something that you can remove with a tweezers, do so, but do not use your fingers as you can accidentally lodge the item further down. If the item is lodged in the throat, try pushing on the dog's abdomen to expel the object.

If dog is not breathing, give him mouth-to-mouth resuscitation (see TIP).

Cuts, Injuries, and Dog Bites

Severe cuts and lacerations will most likely require suturing. Use pressure bandages to slow or stop the bleeding, except in severe crushing injuries. If injuries are severe, such as a car accident, there may be internal bleeding. Use a stiff board to transport the dog, and seek veterinary attention.

Dog bites can cause severe puncture wounds, many of which take a few minutes to appear, so check Rusty over several times. If the wounds are not serious, wash them out with a mild 10 percent betadine/90 percent water mixture. Your veterinarian will want to see the dog and prescribe antibiotics to reduce the risk of abscesses. Check with the owner of the dog that bit your Wheaten to make sure its rabies vaccination is current.

Poisoning

Call your veterinarian and poison control center immediately for the correct course of action. Have the chemical or substance handy so you can properly describe it to a veterinarian or poison control center worker. Do not induce vomiting unless told to do so.

Electrocution

If Rusty is still touching the electricity source, do not touch him or you may be electrocuted also. Use a wooden broom handle or other non-conductive item to unplug the cord. Treat as for shock. Administer mouth-to-mouth resuscitation.

Burns

A severe burn, where the skin is charred or where underlying tissue is exposed, requires immediate veterinary attention. You can treat minor burns over a small area with ice packs or cold water. Do not use water on extensive burns or you may risk shock. Aloe Vera is an effective burn treatment after the burn blisters.

Shock

Signs include pale gums, weakness, rapid, thready pulse, shallow breathing, and general unresponsiveness. Keep Rusty quiet and maintain his body temperature. Seek veterinary attention immediately.

Broken Bones

Fractures to the head, chest, or back may be life-threatening. Keep Rusty quiet and, while trying to keep him stationary, move him onto a flat board where he can remain rigid. Immediately transport him to a veterinarian.

If your Wheaten has broken his leg, you can fashion a splint from a stick, a rolled-up piece of stiff cardboard, or even a rolled-up newspaper. Put the splint alongside the broken leg and wrap either VetWrap or tape around it until you can get veterinary help.

Insect Bites and Stings

You can treat most insect bites and stings with an over-the-counter antihistamine that your veterinarian can recommend. If Rusty shows any allergic reactions to bites or stings, such as severe swelling or difficulty breathing, seek immediate veterinary attention. This can be a life-threatening condition known as an anaphylactic reaction.

Saying Good-bye

At some point in your Wheaten's life, you may have to face the difficult choice of having to euthanize your faithful companion. Euthanasia is painless and quick when administered by your veterinarian. Once you make the decision that Rusty is suffering, take him to your veterinarian for this final act of love. After the euthanasia, you may wish to have Rusty cremated or buried. You may want Rusty's ashes returned to you in an urn, buried in a specially designated pet cemetery, or a mass cremation. Ask your veterinarian for available options.

Don't be ashamed if you are sad or cry over Rusty's death. Your grief is normal. Talk to your veterinarian for a list of pet loss hot lines and support groups in your area or you can find help on the Internet at *http://petloss.com/*.

BREEDING AND SHOWING WHEATENS

Spaying and Neutering

There are many good reasons to spay or neuter your Soft Coated Wheaten Terrier. Besides not contributing to the burgeoning pet overpopulation, spaying or neutering your pet has many health benefits (see below). Overall, you will have a happier, healthier pet when you spay or neuter.

If you purchased your Wheaten from a reputable breeder, chances are the breeder has already made the decision for you. He or she has probably sold the puppy with a limited registration and requirements for spaying or neutering by the time the puppy is six months. The AKC will not register any puppies produced from a dog with limited registration. The puppies may indeed be purebred, but they are completely unregisterable.

Benefits

✔ Reduces or eliminates the risk of certain types of cancers and tumors including (for males) prostate and testicular, (for females) mammary, uterine, and ovarian.
✔ Eliminates the urge to roam looking for mates.
✔ Prevents unwanted litters; makes you a responsible owner.
✔ Can reduce aggression in both sexes.

Spaying or neutering your Wheaten Terrier will make a happier, healthier pet.

✔ In females, eliminates the risk of contracting pyometra, a potentially fatal condition in which the uterus becomes infected.
✔ In females, eliminates the heat cycle, which can occur as frequently as once every three months.
✔ Can make your Wheaten more attentive and responsive to you; can help eliminate behavioral problems.

If Your Wheaten Accidentally Becomes Pregnant

Suppose you've delayed spaying Bonnie and she comes into heat. You didn't notice and come home to a strange dog in your yard mated to her. Or perhaps she has suddenly become very fat two months after her heat. You think she's pregnant. What do you do? You have three possible options: spaying, mismate shots, or carrying the puppies to term.

Spaying: If your Soft Coated Wheaten Terrier is pet quality or very young—under 1½ years old—the best course is to spay her. The gestation period for puppies is about 63 days; do not delay the decision to spay her. Many veterinarians dislike spaying pregnant bitches, especially those that are near term, but it will be more expensive, and more complications will develop the longer you wait. If your Wheaten is accidentally pregnant, spay now.

Mismate shot: If Bonnie is show quality and you must have her intact, your veterinarian can use a mismate shot. Mismate shots are risky and have a high probability of causing pyometria, a life-threatening infection of the uterus. Many veterinarians would rather see the puppies to term than risk pyometra. There are two types of mismate shots: a "morning after" variety, and a shot that will work up to 45 days. The morning after variety is very toxic and can lead to a fatal anemia. Obviously, the sooner your veterinarian uses the mismate shot on your Wheaten, the more effective it is; still, there is no guarantee it will work.

Carrying to term: If your Wheaten is a show-quality dog, having her carry the puppies to term may be the only low-risk solution.

Showing Your Soft Coated Wheaten Terrier

If Bonnie proves to be show quality, you may want to consider showing her in American Kennel Club (AKC) dog shows. At these shows, dogs compete for such titles as Best of Breed and Best in Show. The most coveted title for nonchampions is the Winner's Dog or Winner's Bitch where the dog earns points toward its championship.

Check with the AKC for a listing of dog shows in your area. Contact other Soft Coated Wheaten Terrier breeders and the local breed club to find out more about these shows. The biggest show for terriers is the Montgomery County Kennel Club show, where all the terriers have their national specialties in conjunction. Contact the SCWTCA for more information.

You cannot simply enter a show and appear on the show date. You will first have to learn to stack your Wheaten—position her so as to show off her best qualities—and how to handle her properly in the show ring. You will also have to learn how to groom a Wheaten for the show ring. Many owner-handlers go to conformation training classes to learn the proper way to handle a dog. Many professional obedience trainers also teach handling for the show ring.

Dog Shows

Conformation dog shows are not just "beauty pageants." The AKC intends them to be shows for reputable breeders to display their breeding stock and to demonstrate how well they conform to the Standard; therefore, you cannot show a neutered or spayed dog except in the veterans' class at a specialty show.

The AKC has other shows in which you can enter your neutered or spayed dog. These include obedience, tracking, and agility trials.

Breeding Considerations

Should You Breed Your Soft Coated Wheaten Terrier?

With so many mediocre purebred dogs, you should consider breeding your Soft Coated Wheaten Terrier only if your dog will improve the breed. You should be able to answer "yes" to the following questions before considering breeding your Soft Coated Wheaten Terrier.

✔ Is your dog an exemplary model of the Wheaten Standard?

✔ Do you understand the Soft Coated Wheaten Terrier AKC Standard and Amplification as published by the SCWTCA?

✔ Are you familiar—in person or through photographs—with the relatives of your Soft Coated Wheaten Terrier?

✔ Did you buy your Wheaten from a reputable breeder who sold it as show quality?

✔ Do breeders in good standing with SCWTCA consider your Wheaten to be show quality?

✔ Does your Wheaten have its championship or is she at least pointed, or has she had obedience, tracking, or other titles of merit?

✔ Does your Wheaten have renal dysplasia? Is she definitely not a known carrier of RD, with no marker gene present, and has she been tested?

✔ Is she free from PLE/PLN and is there no incidence in her parents or siblings?

✔ Has your Wheaten been OFA-certified Good or Excellent hips?

✔ Has she received her CERF certification?

✔ Will breeding your Wheaten improve the breed?

✔ Will you guarantee the health of the puppies and refund or replace an unsound puppy?

✔ Are you willing to take back a puppy, regardless of age or condition?

✔ Will you interview and find suitable homes for the puppies?

✔ Will you require spay/neuter contracts and limited registrations?

✔ Will you have a contract requiring that the owners take proper care of their Wheaten?

✔ Are you willing to keep *any* or *all* puppies if you cannot find suitable homes for them? Remember, Wheatens are not popular dogs and you may have difficulty placing puppies in appropriate pet homes.

The Cost of Breeding a Bitch

Breeding dogs is an expensive business. Most breeders make little or no money when breeding their dogs. Consider the following expenses:

✔ Stud fee: $500+

✔ Veterinary exams, wormings, vaccinations, vaginal smears, and other incidental veterinary care: $300–$1,000

✔ OFA, CERF, certification against renal dysplasia: $100–$250

✔ Whelping at veterinarian: $300–$800

✔ Caesarian section or other emergency procedures: $500+

✔ Extra puppy food: $150+

✔ Whelping box, heat lamps or heating pads, other miscellaneous items: $200+

✔ Puppies' vaccinations (six puppies): $200–$400

✔ Puppies' wormings (six puppies): $100

✔ Emergency procedures for puppies: $200+

✔ Ads, phone calls to place pups: $20–$150

✔ Puppy packages (six pups): $60–$100

✔ Other miscellaneous expenses: $100+

✔ Time off from work to care for mother and puppies: 10 weeks × (4–16 hours a day) × (dollars per hour). Even if you do not work, consider dollar per hour to be at least the minimum wage.

TIP

Line Up Puppy Buyers

Line up prospective puppy buyers before the puppies are born. Have them look at your contract and ask questions now. Soft Coated Wheaten Terriers produce six puppies on average, although the number can go as high as ten or as low as one.

Preventive Maintenance

You should have your veterinarian give your Wheaten a thorough physical exam before breeding him or her. The health of the female is especially important. She should be in the peak of health and not too fat or thin. You should renew her vaccinations before breeding her to give the puppies added immunity. The stud dog should be fit and active as well. Your veterinarian should test both dogs for brucellosis, a form of canine venereal disease that will cause miscarriages and failures to conceive in the female and infertility in the male.

Choosing a Bitch or Dog to Breed to Your Soft Coated Wheaten Terrier

Now that you've established that your Soft Coated Wheaten Terrier is show quality and free of hereditary diseases, you must find a suitable mate. You should hold your Wheaten's prospective mate to the same standards. It should be AKC-registered, conform to the standard, and be certified free of hereditary

Spay or neuter your Soft Coated Wheaten Terrier. With so many mediocre purebred dogs, you should only breed if your Wheaten is an AKC Champion or is at least pointed. Both dogs should be screened free from genetic diseases.

diseases. It should also complement any faults that your Wheaten might have. For example, if your Wheaten bitch's ears are slightly low set, your should choose a stud dog with excellent ears.

Unless your neighbor shows Soft Coated Wheaten Terriers, don't choose a dog nearby. Never choose your Wheaten's mate for the sake of convenience; your neighbor's dog is likely to be a product of backyard breeding or puppy mills.

Mating

Either the stud or the bitch should be experienced; otherwise, you may have hours of little productivity. You should not leave your dogs to perform alone; this could result in injured animals, especially if either dog shows aggression or panics during the "tie."

The female is usually receptive between about the tenth through the eighteenth day into her estrus (heat cycle). She will ovulate sometime during this period. She will stand for the male and exhibit a behavior called "flagging." If she sits down and growls or snaps if the male tries to approach her, she is not ready. Do not force a breeding on an unreceptive female. Your veterinarian can help you determine her readiness with vaginal smears. Morning breeding attempts, before either dog has eaten breakfast, are usually the most successful.

Once the dogs mate, either naturally or with your help, they will tie. This tie can last anywhere from a few minutes to an hour. During the tie, the male will usually turn by putting both front feet on the ground and turning completely around until the two dogs are standing tail to tail. Keep both dogs still during this time to avoid panicking and injury. Do not try to pull them apart as this will injure the dogs. Let the tie finish naturally.

Breed your bitch every day or every other day until she refuses to stand for the male.

Pregnancy and Gestation

Most veterinarians are able to determine pregnancy between the twenty-first to thirty-fifth day through palpating the female. Palpating before the twenty-first day or after the thirty-fifth day is unreliable. Ultrasound can also determine if the female is pregnant.

The puppy gestation cycle is generally 63 days. To calculate when the puppies will be born, breeders add 63 days to the date of the first tie.

Nutritional Requirements of the Bitch

Feed your Wheaten female premium high-protein dog food. Many breeders will switch the female to puppy food to provide enough nutrition for the mother and the whelps. For the first month, feed her a normal ration of the high-quality food. Keep her trim and active; an overweight female can have complications

This Wheaten dam takes loving care of her puppies.

associated with whelping. During the last month, feed your Wheaten female 1½ times her normal ration of a premium high-protein dog food.

Whelping

As the sixty-third day approaches, the bitch may start growing anxious. She may search for a suitable place to whelp her pups—in a closet, underneath the porch, or under your bed. You should have a whelping box big enough for her and her pups with a "pig rail" (a small strip of wood) and shelf to keep the newborns from crawling into corners. Place the box in a warm,

CHECKLIST

Items Needed for Whelping
✔ Whelping box, may be made of plastic or wood; it should comfortably fit the mother and her pups
✔ Newspapers to line the whelping box
✔ Soft material to lay over newspapers—newspapers are too slippery for puppy feet. Carpet remnants or mattress pads, with the elastic removed
✔ Heating pad or heat lamps with a rheostat
✔ Puppy nursing kit—bottle, milk replacement
✔ K-Y jelly
✔ Hemostat and scissors
✔ Betadine
✔ Rubber surgical gloves
✔ Clean towels
✔ Rectal thermometer

quiet room, away from normal activity, and introduce her to the box.

Most puppies are born between the fifty-ninth and sixty-sixth days. She should begin losing hair around the nipples and abdomen and her mammary glands should start to fill with milk a few days before whelping. Beginning with the fifty-fifth day, you should begin checking the bitch's temperature once every 12 hours. A two-degree drop in temperature to 99°F (37.2°C) indicates the puppies will be born within the next 24 hours. While you can miss the temperature drop, if you see this drop, it is a sure indication that you should stay home and wait for the puppies to arrive.

Do not allow a large crowd to be present at the whelping, as this will make the bitch nervous and upset, and if she becomes upset, she could come out of labor altogether. Count each placenta with each puppy. If the bitch does not tear the umbilical cord, you may have to clamp it and cut it yourself. Use a sawing motion, rather than a clean cut to avoid possible bleeding. Dip the end in betadine. In a few days, the umbilical remnants will fall off. Most puppies are born head first, but a large percentage can come out breach.

Obtain veterinary assistance if any of the following situations arise:
✔ A puppy is stuck in the birth canal.
✔ The bitch has prolonged labor (30 minutes) and no puppy appears.
✔ The bitch has mild or intermittent contractions for over two hours.
✔ There is a bloody, foul-smelling, or puslike (yellowish) discharge.
✔ The bitch has stopped labor or is exhausted and there are still more puppies inside.

✔ The bitch does not give birth 24 hours after the temperature drop.

✔ Anything simply looks wrong or out of the ordinary.

Newborn Puppy Care

1. Once each puppy is born, present each one to the bitch to allow her to cuddle and clean them. This will help the mother bond with the puppy and recognize each puppy's scent.

2. Allow the puppy to nurse. If the litter is especially large or if the mother is sick, you may have to supplement with puppy milk replacer, readily available in pet supply stores and through catalogs. If the puppies are orphaned, or the mother cannot feed them, the puppies will require feedings every two hours until they are about three weeks. They should be healthy, without diarrhea.

3. Newborn puppies cannot regulate their temperature and will chill easily. Have a heat lamp or specially designed heating pad with a rheostat for newborn puppies.

Warning: Heating pads for humans are too hot and may burn the puppies.

4. Healthy puppies are generally quiet. If the puppies are screaming or crying, something may be wrong and you should seek veterinary help. Puppies that do not move or are too quiet may also be sick. Have your veterinarian examine the mother and puppies within the first two or three days after the puppies' birth. Have him or her remove dewclaws at this time.

5. Puppies' eyes open at about ten days to two weeks; teeth emerge somewhere around the third week. Talk to your veterinarian about worming them at this time. Your veterinarian can prescribe a gentle wormer that will remove roundworms and hookworms.

6. At three to four weeks, you can begin to wean. Start the puppies on a diet of mashed soaked puppy food and milk. If the puppies do not eat, entice them by offering them some food on your fingertip.

7. Socialize your puppies by holding them and petting them. They need to learn that humans are their friends and they should allow being handled.

8. Do not allow your Wheaten puppies to leave their mother any earlier than eight weeks old. They need the time to learn how to be dogs from their mother and siblings.

9. The puppies will need their first vaccinations by the time they are six weeks old. They will need subsequent vaccinations approximately every three weeks until they are sixteen weeks old to ensure immunity against deadly canine diseases (see pages 71–75). At eight weeks, the puppies are mature enough to leave home with their new owners.

Provide a packet for the new owners including contracts, registration, care instructions, puppy food, and health certificates. Many breeders like to include a pet owner's manual such as this one and a toy as part of the puppy package. Be certain to emphasize the responsibilities of pet ownership and offer any help if they have difficulties.

INFORMATION

Organizations

The Soft Coated Wheaten Terrier Club of
 America
Corresponding Secretary, Genie Kline
585 Timberlane Road
Wetumpka, AL 36093
SCWTCA Public Information Hot Line
 (650) 299-8778
 Note: The SCWTCA offers a breeder referral
service at no cost. Contact the SCWTCA at their
hot line number for more information.

The American Kennel Club
5580 Centerview Drive, Suite 200
Raleigh, NC 27606
Phone: (919) 233-9767
Fax: (919) 233-3740
e-mail: info@akc.org

National Rescue—United States
Dana Frady
2316 Brown Bark Drive
Beavercreek, OH 45431
Home phone: (513) 429-7057
Work phone: (937) 253-6464
e-mail jendu@worldnet.att.net

National Rescue—Canada
Soft-Coated Wheaten Terrier Rescue
Pat Cooper
Box 387
Sharon, Ontario
Canada L0G 1V0
Phone: (905) 770-9831

Orthopedic Foundation for Animals
2300 Nifong Boulevard
Columbia, MO 65201
Phone: (314) 442-0418

The World Wide Web

These URLs are for reference only and the author makes no guarantees as to the accuracy
or validity of anything on these web pages.

The Soft Coated Wheaten Terrier Club of America	http://www.scwta.org
Soft Coated Wheaten Terrier Association of Canada	http://www.jb-ccs.com/scntac
AKC Web Site	http://www.akc.org/
American Working Terrier Association	http://www.dirt-dog.com/awta/index.shtml
CERF Web Site	http://www.vet.purdue.edu/~yshen/cerf.html
North American Dog Agility Council	http://www.nadac.com/
OFA Web Site	http://www.offa.org/
UKC Web Site	http://www.ukcdogs.com/
United States Dog Agility Association	http://www.usdaa.com/
VetGen Web Site	http://www.vetgen.com/

Canine Eye Registry Foundation
Department of Veterinary Clinical Science
School of Veterinary Medicine
Purdue University
West Lafayette, IN 47907
Phone: (765) 494-8179
Fax: (765) 494-9981

Periodicals

Benchmarks
The Quarterly Publication for the Soft Coated
  Wheaten Terrier
Contact the SCWTCA
Corresponding Secretary, Genie Kline
585 Timberlane Road
Wetumpka, AL 36093
SCWTCA Public Information (650) 299-8778

Dog Fancy
Subscriptions
P.O. Box 53264
Boulder, CO 80322-3264
Phone: (303) 666-8504

Books—Soft Coated Wheaten Terrier

The Soft Coated Wheaten Terrier Club of Amer-
  ica. *The Soft Coated Wheaten Terrier Owner's
  Manual,* 1984.
Vesley, Roberta A. *The Complete Soft Coated
  Wheaten Terrier.* New York: Howell Book
  House, 1991.
———. *The Soft Coated Wheaten Terrier: Coat of
  Honey Heart of Gold.* New York: Howell Book
  House, 1999.
  You can purchase other publications by the
Soft Coated Wheaten Terrier Club of America
through the SCWTCA.

Books—General Reference

American Kennel Club. *The Complete Dog Book,*
  19th Edition Revised. New York: Howell Book
  House, 1997.

Baer, Ted. *Communicating with Your Dog.*
  Hauppauge, NY: Barron's Educational Series,
  Inc., 1989.
Bailey, Gwen. *The Well-Behaved Dog.* Haup-
  pauge, NY: Barron's Educational Series, Inc.,
  1998.
Benjamin, Carol Lea. *Second-Hand Dog.* New
  York: Howell Book House, 1988.
Carlson, Delbert G., and James M. Griffin.
  *The Dog Owner's Home Veterinary
  Handbook.* New York: Howell Book House,
  1992.
Coffman, Howard D. *The Dry Dog Food Refer-
  ence.* Nashua, NH: Pig Dog Press, 1995.
Collins, Donald R. *The Collins Guide to Dog
  Nutrition.* New York: Howell Book House,
  1987.
Holst, Phyllis A. *Canine Reproduction, A
  Breeder's Guide.* Loveland, CO: Alpine Publica-
  tions, 1985.
James, Ruth B. *The Dog Repair Book.* Mills, WY:
  Alpine Press, 1990.
Klever, Ulrich. *The Complete Book of Dog Care.*
  Hauppauge, NY: Barron's Educational Series,
  Inc., 1989.
Merck and Co. *The Merck Veterinary Manual,*
  Seventh Edition. Whitehouse Station, NJ:
  Merck and Co., Inc., 1991.
Papurt, M. L. *Saved! A Guide to Success with
  Your Shelter Dog.* Hauppauge, NY: Barron's
  Educational Series, Inc., 1997.
Ralston Purina Company. *Purina's Complete
  Guide to Nutrition, Care, and Health for Your
  Dog and Cat.* St. Louis, MO: Ralston Purina
  Company, 1998.
Rice, Dan. *The Complete Book of Dog Breeding.*
  Hauppauge, NY: Barron's Educational Series,
  Inc., 1996.
Smith, Cheryl S. *Pudgy Pooch, Picky Pooch.*
  Hauppauge, NY: Barron's Educational Series,
  Inc., 1998.

About the Author

Margaret H. Bonham is a professional freelance writer. She has been training and breeding dogs since 1987. Her writing has appeared in *Dog Fancy, Pet Life, Pet View, Dog and Kennel, Mushing Magazine, ISDRA Info, Natural Pet,* and *Appaloosa Journal.* She writes the agility column in *Dog and Kennel* called "Obstacles of Course."

Photo Credits

Isabelle Francais: pages 2-3, 8 right, 12, 16, 17 left, 20, 36, 48, 60, 76, 84; Tara Darling: pages 4, 8 left, 9 top, 21, 28 bottom left, 29, 33 bottom right, 40, 41 top right, 41 bottom right, 52 bottom, 56 top, 57, 68, 72 top left, 72 bottom left, 88; Toni Tucker: pages 9 bottom, 17 right, 24, 28 top left, 32, 33 top right, 33 bottom left, 56 bottom, 73, 89; Kent and Donna Dannen: pages 45, 52 top; Pets by Paulette: page 53; Barbara Augello: pages 64, 65.

Cover Credits

Front cover: Pets by Paulette; Inside front cover: Isabelle Francais; Inside back cover: Kent and Donna Dannen; Back cover: Isabelle Francais.

Important Note

This pet owner's guide tells the reader how to buy and care for a Soft Coated Wheaten Terrier. The author and the publisher consider it important to point out that the advice given in the book is meant primarily for the normally developed puppies from a reputable breeder; that is, dogs of excellent physical health and good temperament.

Anyone who adopts a fully grown Soft Coated Wheaten Terrier should be aware that the animal has already formed its basic impressions of human beings. The new owner should watch the dog carefully, including its behavior toward humans, and should meet the previous owner. If the dog comes from a shelter, it may be possible to get some information on the dog's background and peculiarities.

There are dogs that, for whatever reason, behave in an unnatural manner, or may even bite. Under no circumstances should a known "biter" or an otherwise ill-tempered dog be adopted or purchased as a pet or show prospect.

Caution is further advised in the association of children with dogs, in meeting with other dogs, and in exercising the Soft Coated Wheaten Terrier without a leash.

Even well-behaved and carefully supervised dogs sometimes do damage to someone else's property or cause accidents. It is therefore in the owner's interest to be adequately insured against such eventualities.

Dedication

To Larry, who patiently endures the dog madness. And to Al and Betty Holowinski, who taught me the love of books.

Acknowledgments

Special thanks go to the following people and organizations (in no particular order): The Soft Coated Wheaten Terrier Club of America, the American Kennel Club, Pat Donahue, Neil O'Sullivan, Donna Rogers, Nona Mansfeld, Annette Stumf, DVM, Caroline Coile, Susan Conant, Charlene LaBelle, Larry Bonham, Betty Holowinski, Karen Holowinski, Mark Miele, Grace Freedson, and Deborah Schneider.

All inquiries should be addressed to:
Barron's Educational Series, Inc.
250 Wireless Boulevard
Hauppauge, NY 11788
http://www.barronseduc.com

International Standard Book No. 0-7641-1312-7

Library of Congress Catalog Card No. 99-35914

Library of Congress Cataloging-in-Publication Data
Bonham, Margaret H.
    Soft coated wheaten terriers : a complete pet owner's manual / Margaret H. Bonham.
      p. cm.
    Includes bibliographical references.
    ISBN 0-7641-1312-7 (alk. paper)
    1. Soft coated wheaten terrier. I. Title.
SF429.S69B66   2000
636.755—dc21   99-35914
                         CIP

Printed in Hong Kong

9 8 7 6 5 4 3 2